Georgene Denison
1/29/83

ROYAL FAMILY
YEARBOOK

First published in Great Britain 1982 by Colour Library International Ltd.
© **1982 Illustrations and text: Colour Library International Ltd.,**
Guildford, Surrey, England.
Colour separations by LLOVET, Barcelona, Spain.
Display and text filmsetting by ACESETTERS LTD., Richmond, Surrey, England.
Printed and bound in Barcelona, Spain by RIEUSSET and EUROBINDER.

ISBN 0 86283 019 2
COLOUR LIBRARY INTERNATIONAL

D.L.B.:31226-82

ROYAL FAMILY
YEARBOOK

TEXT BY
TREVOR HALL

FOREWORD BY
THE EARL OF LICHFIELD

FEATURING THE PHOTOGRAPHY OF
DAVID LEVENSON & NEIL SUTHERLAND

DESIGNED BY
PHILIP CLUCAS MSIAD

PRODUCED BY
TED SMART & DAVID GIBBON

COLOUR LIBRARY BOOKS

In today's world of instant electronic communication our perception of Royalty is inevitably highly coloured by the media. And given television's predictable infatuation with pageantry, we need not be unduly surprised if the first images that spring to mind are the scenes of spectacular solemnity that we British do so well – the Royal Wedding, the Opening of Parliament, Trooping the Colour.

But we undervalue our Royalty if we think of them as purely a pretext for pomp and circumstance, as no more than a glorious excuse for gilded ceremonial. Because, as this book amply illustrates, our Royal Family is very much a working Royal Family.

For every ermine-edged occasion that catches the eye of the media there are a hundred more mundane tasks performed by each and every member of the Royal Family throughout the year. A factory to be opened here, an old people's home to be visited there, inspecting, admiring, validating with their presence the efforts of thousands of ordinary men and women.

There is, of course, invariably some kind of ceremony associated with these public appearances. Plaques are unveiled, ribbons cut, trees planted. But their true value lies, not in the formal and often gratuitous trimmings, but in the informal, smiling presence of a member of Royalty, a representative of the Establishment, whose interest and attention mark the project out as worthy of note.

Distracted as we tend to be by the bowing and scraping, the shaking of hands and the dropping of curtseys, we sometimes find it difficult to think of these activities as work in the proper sense of the word. Work is Prince Michael of Kent's banking activities, Prince Philip's chairing of endless committee meetings or, more heroically, Prince Andrew's service in the Royal Navy. But hosting garden parties? Touring housing developments? Not exactly hard manual labour, muses the cynic.

Attitudes like that entirely misunderstand the very real effort that goes into such activities, and the very real sense of support that results. Attending a Buckingham Palace garden party as a guest is an enjoyable diversion, but hosting five of them every year, shaking hands, fixing a friendly smile, finding the appropriate small talk – that really is Work.

The events of the last year have focused the spotlight very firmly on what Fleet Street insists on calling our "Fairytale Prince and Princess," a phrase that itself reveals a lot about the image of Royalty the media prefer. But there are other members of the family, each of them making his or her contribution.

Ironically enough, in this age of liberation, it is often the more junior female members of the Royal Family who tend to get less attention than they deserve: Princess Margaret and Princess Anne are always good for a story, but what about Princess Alexandra, the Duchess of Kent, the Duchess of Gloucester. Each serves the public in a hundred different ways throughout the year and each is diligently ignored by all but the local press. Less publicity-worthy, perhaps, because less directly related to the Throne, they nonetheless continue to perform their weekly rota of public functions with dignity and diligence.

Their contribution to the day to day duties of Royalty underlines the fact that the story of the Royal Year is not focused on just a few individuals: it is the story of an entire family.

RT. HON. THE EARL OF LICHFIELD F.I.I.P., F.R.P.S.

JUNE 1981

Where to begin and end any account of a year in the life of the British Royal Family? It is tempting to plump for the calendar year as the safest and most easily recognisable period, but the long and unashamedly leisurely royal vacation at Balmoral provides cogent evidence that the Queen at least sees her public year as starting in October and finishing the following July. There is a case for treating the Queen's official birthday, traditionally celebrated on the second Saturday in June, as the event which divides one year from the next: this was indeed the basis on which the one and only comprehensive and authorised film about a typical royal year – *Royal Family,* shown in the run-up to the Investiture of Prince Charles as Prince of Wales in July 1969 – was produced.

A fixed event like Trooping the

organisers for whom this is truly a once-a-year occasion; the stall-holders whose harvest of customers must be attracted to what they have to sell; the fairground which makes a mint of money out of the fact that the Derby has long since become a family occasion on which children have to be catered for as fully as their parents.

The nervous tension belongs, and is the prerogative of, the small army of owners, trainers, stable-lads, grooms and, by no means least of all, the jockeys. For all of them, an enterprise which began as much as four years before, when the sires and dams of today's runners were mated almost specifically with this occasion in mind, comes to fruition. The result of the race determines not only the destination of almost £200,000 worth of prize money, but also the stud value of every horse

Colour is probably the best candidate of the three, punctuating the year as it does with the unchanging and normally triumphant celebration of a royal tribute by a resplendent militia in full ceremonial dress. Equally unchanging is the annual Derby meeting. Epsom at the beginning of June provides a

focal point, even for just one afternoon, for so many people – royalty and commoners, British and foreign, sporting and spectating, serious-minded and fun-seeking – and we have chosen that event to begin our pictorial chronicle of a year of colourful happenings, both local, national and international, over which the Queen, as Head of

State, and her family in its supporting role have presided. The Derby, held every year on Epsom Downs, has never lost its grip on the public imagination. Off the course and outside the specialised and highly commercial confines of the world of thoroughbred breeding, the event attracts the speculation of millions of ordinary men and women, who on this occasion as on no other sink many more millions of pounds into what is sometimes, if a little unkindly, called the bookmakers' benevolent fund.

On and around the course, the day itself is one of feverish activity and tensed nerves. The feverish activity is that of the

taking part. A victory at this most especial of Britain's five Classic races puts the winner into such demand as a stallion, that £10 million is these days a cheap price to pay for him.

The Queen, seeking the first Derby win for a member of her family in over three quarters of a century, declared her own entry, which she does as often as not. His name was Church Parade and the Queen's reservations about his chances of success seemed to be evidenced by the fleeting, uncertain looks on her normally relaxed features as the proceedings got under way on 3rd June. Appearances had to be kept up, however, and she arrived, accompanied by the

Queen Mother (opposite page, top), smiling brightly as the motorcade crept silently up the course.

Fashion-wise, 1981 seemed to be the year in which deep, bright colours took the place of paler shades and subtle pastels, as the Queen was obviously aware. Red was clearly the royal favourite, with Princess Alexandra wearing almost exactly the same shade as the Queen, in an outfit broken only by a lacy frill which Lady Diana Spencer had already made popular. The Duchess of Gloucester (next to Princess Alexandra in the picture, opposite page, right) wore a similar deep red to set off her pink suit. The Queen's warm, chic cherry-red outfit was one of

weeks brought the five-months-long preparations for the century's most spectacular wedding to its brilliant and triumphal climax. The Queen's tour of Australasia and Sri Lanka found parallels in her son and daughter-in-law's successful visit to their Principality in October, and the news a week later that the new Princess of Wales was expecting her first baby brought an unexpected bonus to this year of celebration, and gave everyone something to look forward to in 1982.

Not that 1982 was short on incident. The quite sudden eruption of the crisis in the Falkland Islands provided the political and patriotic talking point of the year, and the Royal

her personal favourites: she had already worn it at Royal Ascot the previous year, and for her State Visit to Switzerland: it would be seen again in New Zealand in October and at Chichester as late as July 1982. By contrast, the Queen Mother opted for a quiet off-white coat and hat (above) while Princess Michael kept to the bright side

with a crisp, pure-white, close-fitting coat and small saucer-shaped hat (above, far left). These royal fashions could be seen during those few minutes when the Queen and her family came down from the Royal Box to inspect the runners from the side of the course shortly before the Derby itself. The Queen's expression gave nothing away, and she was in events right not to have betrayed too much optimism. Church Parade came fifth – a creditable showing, but one which leaves the Queen with horse-racing ambitions to fulfil.

The 1981 Derby heralded a year of almost unprecedented activity for the Royal Family. Just over a week later came the drama of the now notorious incident during the Trooping the Colour ceremonial, and the following

Family were not isolated from its consequences. From the departure of Prince Andrew in the *Invincible* at the beginning of April to the services of commemoration and charity galas in aid of the dependants of the fallen, the entire Family was in one way or another involved from start to finish.

To crown the success of the campaign, the birth of Prince William justified the national celebration. His christening on 4th August, the Queen Mother's 82nd birthday, provided an apt reminder of the continuity of monarchy and it is for that reason that this first volume of "The Royal Family Yearbook" covers fourteen months instead of the expected twelve.

JUNE 1981

Guards celebrated her official birthday with the annual ceremony of Trooping the Colour.

The day began pleasantly enough, with large crowds – certainly larger than usual even on this occasion – lining the Mall and filling the stands on Horse Guards Parade, ready and waiting to enjoy the almost unchanging ritual at the height of a benign summer's weather. The Queen, mounted side-saddle on her mare Burmese, had stood at the main gates of Buckingham Palace to watch her Guards pass by on their way to Horse Guards, and eventually she took her place in the colourful procession down the

The happy mood of anticipation of the climax of 1981's royal events was startlingly marred by the dramatic events, almost unprecedented this century, which took place on Saturday 13th June – the day on which the Queen's Household Brigades of

Mall, cheered on by thousands of people exuberant with the splendour of the occasion. Just before the procession reached Admiralty Arch, at the Trafalgar Square end of the Mall, it turned right into a short approach road which links the

Mall to Horse Guards Parade. It was at this junction that, as the Queen herself passed, six pistol shots rang out loud and clear from the midst of the crowd. Burmese made an uncontrollable skittish movement which in its suddenness jerked the Queen momentarily off balance, but even riding side-saddle she reacted quickly enough to bring the mare under almost immediate control.

While a mêlée of spectators jostled and fought with the assailant, two or three streetliners – members of the Guards' regiments detailed to line the processional route for the occasion – joined in the fray and dozens of police teemed across the roadway to make their arrest. The procession was thrown into only temporary disorder and continued to make its way to its destination.

Towards its head the Queen, looking quite alarmingly drained

of colour, was giving her mount reassuring pats on the neck, while Prince Charles, who had been riding immediately behind her, trotted up to reassure her that the assailant had been seized.

In fact the man was lucky to be alive at all, such was the outrage felt by nearby spectators and the particular fury of one Guardsman who confessed afterwards to having been so angry that he very nearly used his bayonet on him. As it soon became clear the assault did not amount to an assassination attempt: the pistol fired at or towards the Queen carried only blank rounds, and its owner 17-year-old Marcus Serjeant had, it seemed, intended no harm to the Queen. It transpired, however, during the ensuing criminal trial, in which Serjeant was indicted for firing a gun with intent to alarm the Queen, that he had made several efforts to

obtain live ammunition, had boasted several times to his friends and neighbours that he would do something to make himself famous, and had even written to the Queen to warn her not to leave Buckingham Palace on 13th June as "there is an assassin set up to kill you." He was found guilty and sent to jail for five years.

It was ironic that on this of all occasions the Queen should have been so utterly vulnerable whilst in the presence of such a huge contingent of her personal bodyguard. It was also gratifying that she was so wholly in command of the situation that the procession and the entire ceremony continued without

giving anyone who had not witnessed or heard of the incident the slightest cause for suspicion or unease. For those people, some 8,000 of them, lining the parade ground the military spectacle lived up to expectations throughout, and went on as smoothly as the previous week's rehearsal when Prince Charles took the Salute (left, below left and opposite page top centre). It had the bonus, of course, of being preceded by the usual royal ceremonial arrivals: the Queen Mother and Princess Margaret in one landau and Prince Andrew and Lady Diana Spencer in the other. And the crowds at Buckingham Palace

end knew nothing as they cheered the Queen back to the Palace, and again when she came out onto the balcony (opposite page, centre) for the traditional R.A.F. fly-past. The Queen showed no tension either, as she was joined by some of the younger members of her family – Lord Nicholas Windsor, son of the Duke of Kent, and Lady Davina Windsor and her brother the Earl of Ulster, the children of the Duke of Gloucester.

JUNE 1981

The Most Noble Order of the Garter is the oldest Order of Chivalry in the Kingdom. It was founded in 1348 by King Edward III as a fusion of the two ideals upon which he of all monarchs genuinely strove to establish a stable régime – military strength and religious fervour. Membership of the Order was then confined to the twenty-five most outstanding military leaders, who remained in close fellowship with their Sovereign and with each other for the rest of their days. But the three-day gathering each year – originally around St George's Day on 23rd April, brought them together personally for religious worship "to the honour of Almighty God, the glorious Virgin Saint Mary and St George the Martyr."

Like most ceremonies of ancient origin, the Garter has been the subject of neglect, change and rejuvenation throughout the six centuries of its existence. In

Tudor and Jacobean times the Festival was allowed to lapse occasionally and St George's Day was not always chosen as the precise time of celebration. Services for the installation of new Knights were hardly ever held in the entire course of the

nineteenth century. King George V's deep-seated sense of tradition prompted him to reintroduce many of its facets, but it was his son and successor King George VI who, in celebration of the six-hundredth anniversary of the Order's inauguration, arranged for an assembly of Knights to meet, process to and attend a Service at St George's Chapel, Windsor Castle on 23rd April 1948. The ceremony we know today dates from that time, and 1981's

proceedings, held on 15th June, possessed the added attraction of the attendance of Lady Diana Spencer (below, far left and opposite page, top right) who experienced the solemnity and spectacle of the service for the first time. She was accompanied by Lady Susan Hussey (pictured opposite page, bottom, in gold hat), the Queen's senior lady in waiting, who was responsible for preparing Lady Diana for her future role.

JUNE 1981

There are years when it is forgiveable to imagine that Royal Ascot can do quite well without its royalty. It is very often a social beano that has little or nothing to do with horses, and the preoccupation with the size of hats or the length of skirts, the obsession with socialising for its own sake against a mere background of high quality flat racing is not relieved by Fleet Street's continuing search for the catchy news item or the pictorial scoop which satisfies readers' curiosity and panders to exhibitionism. When these elements are not only present but also prominent, the royal presence seems like a respectable covering over a not very professionally-baked cake. But there have been times when the royal flavour has been strong and authoritative. Black Ascot in

1936 was a particularly striking occasion, when anyone who was anyone signified their mourning for the death of King George V not by foregoing Royal Ascot, but by wearing black on all four days of the meeting. There was genuine excitement at Ascot in 1953, not just because it was held in the same month as the Coronation but also because, in the wake of the superb performance put on by the Queen's horse Aureole in the Derby just a fortnight before, the feeling was that this year must surely be the Queen's year on the racecourse.

1981 was another such year because of the appearance of the Royal Family's potential new recruit, Lady Diana Spencer, now within six weeks of her magnificent and historic wedding. Like the Queen and

demure blush, the lowering of the eyes, following rather than leading where behaviour counted most. Fashion-wise she strove not to outshine. On the first day of Royal Ascot, 16th June, she wore a soft mauve and

the Queen Mother, Lady Diana attended the meeting on all four days and there was never any doubting that she was the cynosure of all eyes. Whether this was through envy, curiosity, protectiveness or admiration mattered not. She had arrived and to prove it she was there. But she maintained the modest, restrained attitude – the famous

gold striped outfit with a plain, semi-platter hat trimmed with ostrich feather (above) – one of her favourite types of adornment in 1981, under the Belleville Sassoon influence. On the second day (top left) she was in an equally delicate peach top and skirt, and sporting a generous fold of material round the neck as a variation of the frill

while Prince Charles was away. He had to miss the middle two days of the meeting in order to pay a visit to the United States to attend a charity gala. But Lady Diana's training for her future role was nothing if not thorough, and when Prince Charles was not available Princess Alexandra (below left) or a personal detective (opposite page far left) or the Queen Mother (overleaf) was. Few public events offered more opportunity to accustom oneself to the sight of huge, admiring, scrutinising crowds, and if Lady Diana harboured any doubts about her ability to cope in front of so many thousands they were dispelled during this one week of Royal Ascot. She was the universal favourite. Prince Charles had picked well.

or ruff which she had already made her hallmark. Day three saw her in a sharp, striking ensemble – bright red lightweight clothes, setting off an expansive candy-striped blouse with a huge bow finishing off another broad, flat ruff (opposite page far left). And on the last day she wore a more subdued dress in blue and white squares with a light, saucer-shaped hat tied down in the Edwardian style with net brought under the chin (above and right). No extremes of fashion here, but a million tall girls up and down the country thanked her for making the flat shoe almost a status symbol. It may have raised some eyebrows that Lady Diana continued to attend Royal Ascot

JULY 1981

It was only natural that Lady Diana should appear to have eclipsed the Royal Family, who themselves turned out in force for Royal Ascot. She had, after all, enjoyed (in the most neutral sense of the word) enormous choice typical of someone basically unsure of herself in her new surroundings. They also mistook her amusing interludes with children and fits of giggling on royal walkabouts as signs that she could not cope with the

publicity since the very earliest days of her courtship almost a year previously; and the great publicity machine, to some extent and understandably encouraged by the Palace in preparation for the Wedding of the Century, had not yet produced all it was capable of in terms of the projection of this new celebrity onto the national screen.

Because of her background and her lifestyle she was portrayed as one in need of protection, vulnerable and fragile, about to be thrown in at the deep end. Those who did not admire her daringly low-cut black taffeta evening gown on her first official appearance considered the

formality of her future life, and they found her choice of clothes precociously mature.

By May, when visits like the one to Broadlands made it clear that she had no intention of changing her ways and that, moreover, the public liked what they saw, the general attitude changed, and the reams of advice which commentators in the Press had been dispensing liberally and often began to peter out. She was at last becoming unques-tioningly accepted and very, very popular. No wonder all eyes were upon her as Society's most colourful race-meeting got underway.

Nevertheless her future in-laws were also there and gave Ascot

its unforgettable and almost unchangeable degree of status. If Royal Ascot is the by-word for massive hats, however, it can be stated authoritatively that none of this reputation can be traced to the Royal Family. As these pictures show, its members attend stylishly, as the occasion demands, but in the same or similar outfits to those worn to any official function. The Queen's blue dress and matching hat with its white camelia (top right) would thus be seen twice on her forthcoming Australasian tour; Princess Margaret's ensemble, topped with a white-plumed turban (above) would be worn, most appropriately, at the celebrations to mark the King of Swaziland's sixty years' reign in September, and the Queen Mother wore the same sunny yellow outfit (right) at a service for the Friends of St Paul's Cathedral in July.

But then, the Royal Family comes to Ascot to enjoy the racing much more than to indulge in fashionable escapades. It is a dyed-in-the-wool family tradition which even Prince Philip, who (opposite page centre left) rarely looks entirely at ease there, is content to acknowledge by his occasional presence.

occasion will be remembered, thanks to the meticulous arrangements by Lord Maclean, for going exactly according to plan, for the superb selection of music chosen by the royal couple and for the faultless timing of every element in the complex timetable of procedures. Security was necessarily strong but pleasantly unobtrusive; arrests took place in single figures only, and for deeds no more anarchic than street-trading or pickpocketing. The seventy-minute-long service, held, unlike any comparable royal wedding since 1501, in St Paul's Cathedral, crystallised everything

The wedding of the Prince and Princess of Wales on 29th July 1981 outshone all previous royal events, with the possible exception of the Queen's Coronation, in terms of colour, spectacle, the acknowledgement of tradition and the depth and sincerity of popular acclaim. In a year which had seen its fair share of domestic troubles the

memorable: the fluffed lines from bride and groom, the Speaker's melodramatic reading of the Lesson, the Archbishop's short address, as cleverly designed as his new ice-blue cape and mitre, the restless fidgeting of the younger bridesmaids, the gradual relaxation in the Queen's demeanour, the occasional tear on the Queen Mother's cheek. Like all wedding days it was very much the bride's hour, and her superb puffed dress of ivory silk encrusted with a thousand sequins and mother of pearl embedded in fussy lace panels and frills, reinforced her claim to popular attention. As Lady Diana she was cheered to the echo on leaving Clarence House in the Glass Coach, and as Princess of Wales the return journey was positively deafening. The symbol and one lasting memory of the day was the now

celebrated balcony kiss – a rare moment of royal spontaneity on a formal occasion. The official photographs were much more studied, for the most part, though Lord Lichfield captured a couple of moments of sheer fun. And balloons on the going-away carriage extended the sense of fun to the end.

AUGUST 1981

The honeymoon began at Broadlands. No pictures exist save those taken privately on the last morning of the stay; some of them are on display at the mansion itself. No concession was made to the demands of publicity after the most public of courtships and the most universally witnessed of weddings. Three days of peace and serenity on English soil were all the Prince and Princess asked and, in the haven which great-uncle Mountbatten had made his own, and where his nephew the Duke of Edinburgh had taken his bride in 1947, the royal couple got it. Around them was

indeed a large part – was for the couple personally but there could be no doubt that the islanders were taking every opportunity to reaffirm their British sympathies in the face of Spanish attempts to take control of Gibraltar and the refusal of King Juan Carlos to attend the Royal Wedding in protest against this very day's proceedings. The 40-minute drive to the quayside in a borrowed Triumph Stag was an emotional experience for everyone (bottom left) and the farewells were sincere and quite moving (below, and bottom pictures). Alone at last they spent twelve days

a strong security presence: within they were with discreet friends and had the use of a 6,000-acre estate in the heart of Hampshire.

On 1st August they travelled to Eastleigh Airport to fly to Gibraltar for the beginning of the foreign leg of the honeymoon. Prince Charles piloted an Andover of the Queen's Flight, leaving his wife as a passenger in the same way that he had, it was rumoured, left her at Broadlands one morning while he went fishing for trout in the Test.

The flight lasted four hours and the royal arrival was wildly feted in a town vibrant with red white and blue. Part of the welcome –

soaking up the sun and visiting one Mediterranean island after another from the Royal Yacht *Britannia* (opposite page top). They swam and windsurfed, toured and explored until on 12th August they reached Egypt as guests of the ill-fated President Sadat. Seven weeks after they took their leave, he was dead, and Prince Charles was again in Cairo to pay his last respects.

But all were unsuspecting at Balmoral when on 19th August the Prince and Princess met the Press at the Brig O'Dee (this page). And even the Princess agreed that it was "one of the best places in the world."

SEPTEMBER 1981

The Queen began her eighth visit to Australia since the beginning of her reign in 1952, on 26th September. For once unaccompanied by the Duke of Edinburgh, who was on a visit to West Germany, she was greeted alone as she left her aircraft, a Boeing 707 of the Royal Australian Air Force, on the VIP Apron at Melbourne Airport. Although the Queen was in cheerful spirits as she arrived at Melbourne, there was no denying the stringent security measures surrounding her. Apart from those with grudges against what they may have seen as royal favour towards a Conservative-led government, there was no shortage of potential threats against the Queen's safety. The Aboriginal Activists' long campaign for native rights was in the ascendant, the IRA have strong support in Melbourne, and the National Front is well represented. The years-old confrontation between groups supporting various followings in South Africa threatened to surface again.

It was hardly surprising therefore that when the Queen attended the Scots Church (left and bottom right) on 27th September for Divine Service, the first of several bomb scares

should have marred the proceedings. It turned out to be a hoax, but it brought out the Bomb Squad, the sniffer dogs and large numbers of extra police, and the crowds diminished as many sightseers left the area for fear of potential danger. But during the service the Minister, Rev Norman Pritchard, said: "Ma'am, I assure you of our abiding loyalty," and the crowds who remained to sing "God Save the Queen" as she left the church proved it.

The first three days of the Queen's visit were full of public engagements. On 28th September she lunched with members of the Order of Australia Association, visited the Commonwealth Conference Centre, and watched the ballet "Onegin" at St Kilda. On the 29th she visited the Caulfield Racecourse (opposite page, top right) which was beautifully decorated out with £1,400 worth of carnations, where she admired the valuable equestrian paintings housed in its museum. Most of the following days were given over to private meetings with Commonwealth Prime Ministers, but by the 5th October the Queen, joined six days earlier by Prince Philip, had sailed to Tasmania to attend Hobart Combined Schools Athletics Meeting (this page). She received a tremendously warm welcome in an atmosphere noticeably more relaxed than at Melbourne.

At the earlier welcoming

SEPTEMBER 1981

ceremony at the Town Hall she noted how much the town had changed since her first visit in 1953 and said she could remember when much of it was green hillside and bushland. Now, in the still comparatively open spaces of the Domain Athletics Centre she chatted with those to whom she awarded medals and received the usual

Australasian tour. They had just been entertained at a reception at Perth's Council House and were on their way to lunch at Government House, a hundred yards or so away. Security was again strict, even though the threats which had characterised the Melbourne visit were conspicuous by their absence. But the Queen insisted that the

mass of posies as she arrived and left. The same day she visited a Rehabilitation Centre and a Police Academy and attended a reception given by the Government of Tasmania. On 8th October the Queen and Prince Philip met the people of Perth during one of their familiar walkabouts, the origin of which dates back to the 1970

walkabout should go ahead as planned and showed no signs of tension as she received local dignitaries (left) and chatted with large crowds of spectators (top). As always she was overwhelmed with flowers from children eager to make this their special day (above). One little girl presented her with a bunch of red roses and asked the

Queen if she could kiss her. The Queen politely refused.
After lunch the Queen changed into an ice blue outfit with a navy blue straw hat to attend a garden party in the grounds of Government House (see previous pages), preceded by an inspection of Scouts, Guides and members of the Girls' and Boys' Brigades who gained the

over the Commonwealth in private, twenty-minute audiences on board the Royal Yacht *Britannia* as she lay at Station Pier some 20 miles from the Australian capital.

Oddly it was the Commonwealth Heads of Government meeting – the catalyst for the Queen's visit – that prompted a degree of criticism which reflected badly on the Queen herself. Complaints over the high cost of putting the meeting on – some estimates set the total cost at up to £13 million – gave the impression of its being an unnecessary extravaganza, and the Queen's dutiful journeying

Queen's Award during 1981. After a private dinner at Government House, the Queen and the Duke of Edinburgh attended a charity performance of the play "Gallipoli," after which they met the stars, executives and production team. Prince Philip spent much of his time with an 86-year-old veteran of the expedition, who kept him engrossed with his reminiscences.

The royal programme in Perth and the way it was carried out contrasted sharply with the six-day visit to Melbourne. That visit was deliberately low-key, partly because of the security aspect and partly because the prime purpose of the visit was to open the Commonwealth Heads of Government Conference. More than half of the Queen's official time in Melbourne was spent meeting each of the 41 heads of government from all

from the other side of the world a rather quaint extension of it. But given that these regular top-level meetings are an indispensible part of member-ship of the Commonwealth, the Queen's presence was, as usual, salutory. Although she did not attend the formal opening ceremony, she had specifically requested to be taken on a tour of the centre in Melbourne

SEPTEMBER 1981

where the meeting would take place, and her own interviews with the various Prime Ministers appear to have helped things along. She certainly impressed Mr Kenneth Kaunda of Zambia, who referred to her at a dinner (at which she was not present) as "our beautiful Queen, composed in mind, beautiful, cool and calm." And one Victorian newspaper combined praise with bluntness in its headline "55-year-old Grandmother Cools The Family Squabbles."

The Duke of Edinburgh went more unobtrusively about his business following his arrival in Melbourne on 30th September. His first solo engagement was a

athletics meeting at Hobart they visited the Douglas Parker Rehabilitation Centre at d'Alton School where the Queen unveiled a plaque and took morning tea with the disabled people. That afternoon the royal couple visited the Tasmania Police Academy at Rokeby where they witnessed a display of police vehicles and equipment in the course of a thirty-minute tour of the building, and in the evening they attended a State reception given by the Government of Tasmania at the Laetare Gardens.

There was another reception the following morning, 6th October, at the Albert Hall in Launceston, given by the Mayor and

lunch at Parkville where he met some hundred heads of various scientific organisations as well as twenty or so past and present Councillors and Honorary Fellows of the Academy of Technological Sciences. The following day he recorded a television interview about the World Wildlife Fund – the Duke had become President of the international organisation five

months earlier. Both this and a subsequent meeting with members of the Australasian Advisory Committee of the Duke of Edinburgh's Commonwealth Study Conferences, were held on board *Britannia*.

A two-day visit to Tasmania marked the beginning of the joint tour by the Queen and Prince Philip. In addition to the

Aldermen of the City, and this was followed by a visit to the National Agricultural Showground where, in addition to seeing some equestrian events and the judging of cattle and sheep, the Queen and Prince Philip were entertained to an impressive, if somewhat amusing demonstration of sheaf-tossing. Not to be outdone, the organisers of the Perth Royal Show hosted the visitors the following day at Claremont, some five miles from Fremantle. They put on a fine, mounted Guard of Honour, a fitting background for this special occasion on which the Queen presented The Queen's Cup to the owner of the winning showjumper (opposite page, top) while the Duke awarded the Gold Cup to the winner of a local qualifying round for the World Cup competition in showjumping. After lunch there, the Queen and Duke toured the areas and stopped to inspect some of the district agricultural displays.

They went their separate ways after this event – the Duke being driven off to St George's Cathedral to unveil the Westminster Abbey Cross, and the Queen travelling directly back to Government House for dinner. She did, however, interrupt her journey quite unexpectedly, for a short stroll in a park, where she was shown some of the local flora (pictures right and below right).

After the following day's engagements in Perth (see pages 22 and 23) the Queen and Prince Philip flew to South Australia for the final three days of their Australian tour. Travelling, as they usually do on such occasions, in an Australian Air Force Boeing 707, they landed at Adelaide airport in the afternoon of 9th October. They were taken immediately to Adelaide Town Hall, where South Australian members of

engagements, the Queen was faced with another reminder of the trouble back home. It was a grisly reminder too, as several groups held up fake coffin lids, representing the hunger-strikers who died in the Maze Prison in Northern Ireland, and shouted, "Brits Out." The Queen, totally used to such behaviour, as she once assured protesting students at Stirling University, ignored the protesters, but the Duke wagged his finger at them in mock displeasure, as if admonishing children. The State reception was as different again, with four hundred people crowding the splendid octagonal room, and fanfares and the strains of the National Anthem punctuating the proceedings.

The following day saw the Queen and Prince Philip undertaking separate engagements. Prince Philip attended a series of high-level meetings and receptions, including one concerning the 1986 World Three-Day Event

the Guards Association provided a Guard of Honour, and where the Mayor and Aldermen entertained them at a brief official reception. A 32-horse mounted police guard then escorted them to Government House where the Governor and Mrs Seaman welcomed them and showed them the Royal Suite on the residence's first floor.

A State reception was held for the Queen and Prince Philip that evening in the Banquet Room of Adelaide's Festival Centre. It was here that, after several days of peaceable

Championship, one involving the presentation of commemorative plaques for the Duke of Edinburgh Award Scheme, a lunch with Trustees of the World Wildlife Fund, the opening of a Swamp Aviary and the presentation of the 1981 Prince Philip Prize for Industrial Design.

The Queen meanwhile spent the morning meeting almost 200 members of the local joint Commonwealth Societies Council before being taken to Adelaide Country Club, a mile or so away, to have lunch with representatives of local ethnic communities. This visit began in typical style, with the Queen walking the hundred yards from the reception area to the Club, past lines of children of all races, dressed in traditional national costume and offering their small gifts of flowers (this page, and opposite page, bottom pictures). Inside, the Queen met 130 guests with whom she had lunch, before leaving for possibly the most interesting – from her personal viewpoint – event of the day, the South Australian Derby Meeting at Morphettville Racecourse. As at Claremont there was an impressive horse-mounted police guard to escort her open Rolls-

Royce down the racetrack to the Members' Stand (opposite page, top left) and she joined a group of twenty-one officials in the Royal Enclosure. She watched three of the afternoon's races, including the fifth race, the Derby itself, and she presented the Cup to the winning owner and put the sash on the winning

horse. Before watching the next race, she also visited the mounting enclosure to meet leading trainers and jockeys. Perhaps it was as well that Prince Philip was elsewhere – although he does not actively dislike horseracing, he was probably much more fascinated by the sight of wallabies, dingoes, koalas and hairy-nosed wombats at the Cleland Conservation Park.

There was a dinner that night at Government House, served in its splendid ballroom. The Archbishop of Adelaide was there to say grace and it was he who the next morning welcomed the Queen and Prince Philip at St Peter's Cathedral for an Ecumenical Service for the Order of Australia Association. Again, IRA supporters were at hand to remind the Queen that ten prisoners had voluntarily starved to death in Belfast, though the abusive reception she received from them was drowned by loyalists who were equally angry at the IRA's latest bomb outrage in London, in which Irish Guardsmen were injured after a nail bomb exploded under a bus carrying them from Chelsea Barracks. But the service went ahead as planned, with the Duke of Edinburgh reading the second Lesson.

Apart from a meeting Prince

Philip had later that morning with members of the Commonwealth Study Conference at Government House, that was the last royal engagement of the Australian tour, and the following morning the Queen and her husband took off from Adelaide Airport for Christchurch, New Zealand. It may well have been felt, at the end of this eighth visit, that the ecstatic atmosphere of the original 1953/4 tour would never be recaptured, and there is much truth in this. But considering how worried the authorities became after the subdued 1963 visit, the Queen

can be gratified that the gradual adaptations she has prompted or approved in the last twenty years have kept the monarchy both relevant and popular half way across the world.

OCTOBER 1981

The Queen and the Duke of Edinburgh did not arrive in New Zealand in the easiest of conditions. After a five-hour flight from Adelaide on board an Air New Zealand DC8 the last thing they wanted was the unwelcoming attentions of one of those high, gusting winds which seem to be regular accompaniments to royal tours of Australasia. But Christchurch International Airport had for hours previously been plagued by them and it was probably some relief to many dignitaries who had been waiting on the tarmac to greet the royal couple, to know that their own ordeal by

weather would soon be over. Ladies had been holding onto their hats and continued to do so as the Queen and Prince Philip stepped out of the aircraft shortly before 5.30 pm on the afternoon of 12th October. The Queen too kept a firm hand on the wide brim of her own pale aquamarine hat as she did so (below right and top picture), venturing to let go only to shake the hand of her official host for the duration of the eight-day visit, New Zealand's Prime Minister, Mr Robert Muldoon (above far right). She was surely mindful of the occasion in 1979 when, while standing during the playing of the National Anthem at the beginning of her State Visit to Oman as the guest of Sultan Qaboos, the wind lifted her hat from her head and only the swiftest of movements on the Queen's part retrieved it before it was lost for ever. At Christchurch Airport she allowed no possibility of a recurrence. Looking conscious of, if not positively angry with, the weather, she performed the inspection of the Royal Guard

(opposite page, top pictures) after the Royal Salute (below left and bottom right). The formalities were over in twenty minutes and the Queen and Prince Philip left in a motorcade (opposite page, bottom right) for Lyttleton, where the Royal Yacht *Britannia* had been berthed since early that morning.

An hour after leaving Christchurch Airport, the Queen was giving a reception on board *Britannia* for the official staff concerned with the royal visit – some 47 members of the Palace staff, and half as many officials from New Zealand – and for the large Press contingent who were covering the tour. Following that, a reception and private dinner were given on board the Yacht, at which the Governor-General, Sir David Beattie and his wife were joined by the Prime Minister and Mr Rowling, the Leader of the Opposition, and their wives.

The Queen has visited New Zealand almost as often as she has been to Australia – for obvious geographic reasons a visit to one is combined with a visit to the other. Happily, the time is long past since a royal visit to New Zealand became synonymous with some natural

or man-made disaster which befell the country during each of the first three visits up to 1970. The most dramatic and saddening of these was the railway accident which occurred on Christmas Eve 1953 and killed several hundred people, and whose effect was so stunning in its immensity that the Queen, giving her Christmas broadcast for the first and only time from outside Britain, felt compelled to refer to it. Since 1970 the coincidences, which at one time seemed so routine that groups of Maoris saw the Queen as a harbinger of ill-luck and agitated for her not to visit New

Zealand again, have stopped. So has the Maori agitation, and although there has in recent years been a certain amount of dissatisfaction with the territorial arrangements with the Maoris, which stemmed from the Treaty of Waitangi of 1840, serious protest against the dominating European presence has been spasmodic and subdued. Certainly New Zealand, always a fairly conformist country, was ready to give the Queen and Prince Philip a sincere and well-organised welcome, in which the Maori community, as we shall see, played its usual, inimitable part.

OCTOBER 1981

The Queen and the Duke of Edinburgh's first full day in New Zealand, 13th October, saw them attending a Service of Thanksgiving at Christchurch Cathedral, to mark its centenary which, strictly speaking, fell on 1st November. The Cathedral (bottom right) is small by comparison to most English examples, and looks in style and position very much like a large parish church in an English provincial town. But it is rich in memorials, boasts a relatively new set of thirteen bells, as well as a beautifully sculptured pulpit with interesting historical panels.

"those famous English entertainers" as he called them, had taken Communion there and only recently Ronnie Corbett had read the Lesson. Among today's congregation were not only the royal visitors but also Mr Muldoon, who took a close personal interest in his Sovereign's tour of the old Dominion, and a group of Maori children who sang an "action song," which added a pleasant touch of informality to this special and dignified service. There was more informality after the service when the Queen and Prince Philip walked past large crowds on their way to Noah's

Unlike the Queen's first day in Australia (and it was noticed that she was wearing the same outfit for her first day in New Zealand) there were no bomb scares, and everything went according to plan on a warm, sunny day. During the service the Dean of Christchurch, the Very Revd M. L. Underhill, said that many famous people had worshipped in the Cathedral, and he listed the most memorable of them – present company excepted, of course: Captain Robert Scott and Sir Ernest Shackleton, two Antarctic explorers, had received God's blessing on their respective ventures; Sir Edmund Hilary and Sir Vivian Fuchs had followed their tradition. At the other extreme, Gert and Daisy –

Navy and become the commander of a ship. "I used to do that," said the Prince, "but these days I'm lucky to stand behind the wheel of *Britannia*." From Noah's Hotel he and the Queen travelled to the Royal New Zealand Air Force base at Wigram for a short flight to Ashburton, the commercial centre of mid-Canterbury and one of the most productive agricultural districts in New Zealand. They lunched at the home of Mr and Mrs Robert Robinson, with its woodlands-style garden stocked with English-type shrubs and trees. Following lunch, an hour's stroll

Hotel for the next part of the day's programme. As these pictures show, the Queen was palpably relaxed and happy as she collected small posies from children lining the route. Prince Philip spoke to one schoolboy who said he wanted to join the through Ashburton Domain, a landscaped arboretum covering some 100 acres in the centre of the town, brought the Queen and Prince Philip within sight of thousands of daffodils and the brilliant colours of azaleas at the peak of their blooms.

The Queen and Prince Philip left Christchurch on the morning of 14th October for Dunedin, towards the southern tip of South Island, for a short but packed programme of engagements. They arrived at noon and within half an hour were in the midst of one of their now habitual walkabouts – one element of a royal visit which was first tried out in New Zealand eleven years before. The walkabout was, for the most

called them "crackpots," and tried to take no notice. "We love the Queen," they said.

The Queen's troubles were not over. Just as she arrived at the Otago Museum, after attending a Civic Luncheon at Dunedin's Southern Cross Hotel, there was a bang, rather like a firecracker. Nobody discovered for certain what it was, and some officials conceded that it may only have been a metal traffic sign being knocked over. The Queen's

police officer, Commander Trestrail, looked worried but the Queen and Prince Philip, who were still in their car when it happened, didn't even seem to hear it, and the visit to the Museum went ahead without delay.

The purpose of today's visit was to inspect the 1981 New Zealand Science Fair with its experimental exhibits showing research and technical skills in the fields of biological and

part, as informal and pleasant as any, with the Queen continually being offered bouquets and posies – and of course accepting them. A particularly special offering came from one lady who showed the Queen a large photograph of the Royal Family in July 1947, taken at the time of the Queen's engagement to Prince Philip (right and above right).

As the royal visitors came towards the end of their walkabout they came face to face with half a dozen or more protest groups – a Maori contingent, some IRA sympathisers, anti-Muldoon protesters, republicans, the unemployed and even lesbians – making a noisy and pointed demonstration against the royal tour and the government who organised it. Their banners referred to "The Empire: Centuries of Struggle and Death," and "Royal State Blunders," and called for "Jobs not Tours." Mr Robert Walton, the Police Commissioner for Dunedin, had to concede that "the people have a right to be there and a right to free speech," but other onlookers

physical sciences, and applied science and technology. The Queen was particularly tickled by a device entitled "Mouse Power," showing mice running almost perpetually on a wheel to produce energy. On a more serious note, the Duke learned that the regional science fairs – there are now thirteen of them in New Zealand – usually involve as many as five thousand exhibitors, young and old, every year.

The visit lasted half an hour, after which the Queen and Prince Philip were driven to Dunedin Airport for a two hour flight to Wellington, on the North Island.

Like many of the Queen's outfits for the Australasian tour, the pale blue coat and hat she wore at Dunedin had been worn already once before. During a visit to the Elphin Showground in the City Park at Launceston, Tasmania only eight days previously she had chosen exactly the same ensemble, with the substitution of the emerald for the pearl brooch (opposite page, top centre and bottom left).

OCTOBER 1981

The royal visit to Wellington lasted for almost forty-eight hours. The first full day was taken up mainly by very formal engagements, with the Duke of Edinburgh presenting his Scheme's Gold Awards at Government House and the Queen presiding at a meeting of the Executive Council at Parliament House. She showed no sign of unease after the previous day's alarms – though it was noticed that she had caught a cold – and thousands of people turned out to cheer her during her ceremonial drive through the City.

After a State luncheon in the Banquet Hall of Parliament House the Queen, who seemed to enjoy her meal of soup,

smoked ham, avocado, steak, pears with crème caramel and cheese, referred to the fact that "my visits with Prince Philip are happily taking place more often. I am here as Queen of New Zealand for the sixth time in my reign and I have the comfortable feeling of being home among friends." She mentioned the forthcoming general elections in New Zealand, and drew laughter when she said, "I have to remain neutral on these occasions but to adapt a well-known saying, the best of New Zealand luck to you all." However much she may have felt among friends, there were more demonstrations that evening as she arrived for a dinner at Government House, when fifty or so people shouted slogans in support of prisoners in Northern Ireland H-block prisons.

The following day, 16th October, the Queen visited Wellington's Town Hall where she held an investiture which included the dubbing of a new knight (pictures left). The Duke of Edinburgh, meanwhile, attended a meeting to select the winner of the Prince Philip Award for Industrial Design. He joined the Queen at the Town Hall later, when they both emerged for a half hour's walkabout (below, below left and opposite page). Then they were on their way to Wellington Airport for the next stage of their tour.

OCTOBER 1981

Auckland's programme began in very much the same way as Wellington's finished – with a walkabout in Queen Street and through Queen Elizabeth II Square. The weather had turned decidedly cool and windy, and showers developed in the course of that first afternoon. But the walkabout was brightened by the usual sight of children

Saturday 17th October was as wet a day as the Queen had yet seen and umbrellas were the order of the day as she reached Auckland Domain to receive the traditional Polynesian welcome. Both she and Prince Philip wore kiwi-feather cloaks to witness the aggressive stampings and chest-beating of the men and the swaying dancing of the

women – all against the background sound of bare feet squelching in mud. One Maori warrior said afterwards – almost spoiling the image – "Gee, I would never let the kids outside in weather like this." Nevertheless the Queen seemed to enjoy the dancing of the groups – Maori, Western Samoan, Nieuan, Tokelauan and

rushing forward to present flowers to the Queen, including one little girl who clutched a huge teddy-bear while doing so – much to the Queen's amusement. There was less amusement in yet another anti-tour demonstration with banners calling for "Brits out now," and "Royal Fat Cats Go Home." But despite that, the welcome in the heart of this conurbation of three quarters of a million people was warm and homely.

Within that population are an estimated 80,000 Maoris and Pacific Islanders, some of them descended from the first settlers who came to New Zealand some three hundred years before the country was first sighted by Tasman in 1642. With their great reputation for the colour, robustness and transparent happiness of their tribal welcomes, the Maoris are an indispensible element in any tour arranged for the Queen.

not true, then the message I have for you is," he continued, "to tell Prince Charles to get on with the job." The Queen laughed openly but with that look on her face as if she could not believe her ears, and made no attempt to comment on the speculation

which would in three weeks be hard news. But she had great praise for the rich cultural heritage of the Pacific Island Communities and the "traditional boldness and sincerity" of their dances. She began and ended her speech

Cook Island – as they formed ranks and files in front of the royal dais. She and the Duke were formally welcomed by the chairman of the New Zealand Maori Council, Sir Graham Latimer, who said that there were rumours that the Queen was about to become a grandmother again. "If that is

with the Maori Salute "kia kaha kia aranui ia tatou" – "All of us here be strong and alert." The royal party spent the following day – a Sunday – at sea, although a dozen members, including the Queen and Prince Philip, left *Britannia* for Motuarohia Island on the east side of the Bay of Islands, for a

barbecue. A perverse stroke of luck suddenly sent the sun from the sky and brought the rain down in such torrents that the barbecue equipment and some of the food was soaked. But Prince Philip helped to cook what could be cooked, and the venture was described as enjoyable.

The two main events of the final complete day were a visit to the Centennial Swimming Pools at Hamilton, which became the excuse for some good-natured fun between children and the royal visitors. Youngsters vied with each other to demonstrate their skills in front of the Queen, and brought her flowers as she passed them. Prince Philip was offered a rosebud and ran after the Queen to show her, gleefully, what he had acquired. They also saw a display of techniques of teaching year-old babies to swim.

Later at Middlepark Stud (these pages) as the Queen saw her filly – named Annie – for the first time. She had been born from the Queen's mare Header who had been sent to the New Zealand stallion Balmerino for mating. The Queen also saw some of her New Zealand stock of Jersey cows (bottom right) which were thriving at the end of a pleasant Summer.

Sri Lanka became a republic ten years ago and severed its last connection with the British monarchy, except through the Commonwealth of which the country acknowledges the Queen as Head. But, contrary to many sentiments expressed in Australia and New Zealand, where ties with the British Royal Family are much stronger, there were no hard feelings about the long gone days of Empire, during the Queen's four day visit made it clear to the Queen that her first visit for 27 years was long overdue. Nor, except within the stout walls of Sri Lanka's Parliament building in Colombo, did the fact that the country was in the grip of a prolonged state of emergency in the face of mounting economic difficulties destroy the festive atmosphere of each one of the four days of the royal visit.

Prince Alfred, the second son of Queen Victoria, was the first

between 21st and 25th October. This was the first time she and Prince Philip had included Sri Lanka on a tour of Australasia since the famous Common-wealth tour of 1953/54 and there was no mistaking the uninhibited and universal welcome accorded to her by all sections of the republic's teeming communities. The photographs on this page show how impossible it was for even the worst weather – at Kandy on 23rd October – to dampen the enthusiasm of townspeople, who

British prince to visit Ceylon, and his welcome in 1870 included an extravagant banquet at which he ate and drank from plate and goblets, and with knives, forks and spoons, all of gold set with rubies, emeralds and pearls. The future King Edward VII visited Ceylon in 1875 and Princess Marie Louise came to its third largest city, Moratuwa, in 1904 and 1906. The Queen and Prince Philip's welcome on 21st October, as they arrived from Perth, Australia in an RAAF Boeing

OCTOBER 1981

707, onto the tarmac at Katunayake International Airport, spot on time at four in the afternoon, was a noisy one as, to a 21-gun salute, the screech of conch-shells, the throb of *magul-bera* and surging cheers from massive crowds they were received by President Jayewardene and his wife (bottom left). The Queen inspected a Guard of Honour (below) to music from the band of the Sri Lankan Navy and bagpipes played by kilted highlanders. The 18 m.p.h. drive to Colombo took them past thousands upon thousands of people standing ten deep in places, cheering madly as the maroon Daimlers approached the Presidential mansion. A State dinner was given that night, prior to which the Queen

of bands from local schools and colleges – girls in colourful saris and boys in crisp white uniforms – giving their musical salutes with tubas, tambourines and trumpets.

The royal visitors left Colombo that evening for a 120-mile journey in the same gleaming, maroon train as they had travelled in in 1954, to Anuradhapura, the holy city revered by all Sri Lankan Buddhists. Leaving their train for a minibus, they were taken to see the sacred Bo tree – planted two thousand years ago from a cutting of the tree under which Buddha himself was reputed to

inspected another Guard of Honour provided by the Sri Lankan Light Infantry. It boasts the largest mascot in the world – a baby elephant called Kandula, caparisoned in the blue fabric, with white plumes, to match the Regiment's colours. On the orders of her mahout, she raised her trunk for the National Anthem and lumbered off in step when the parade was over. At the dinner, the President reviewed the progress of his country's democracy, emphasising the fact that the next day would see the fiftieth anniversary of the granting of the universal franchise. To celebrate it there was a splendid ceremony at Galle Face Green in the centre of Colombo, which the Queen and Prince Philip attended (left) in front of a crowd of almost a million – some 7% of Sri Lanka's entire population. It was a clear, warm day, with the blue-green of the Indian Ocean sparkling in the background as the official speeches were interspersed by the march-pasts

have achieved inner peace. They visited its shrine (for which the Queen discarded her own shoes in favour of a pair of soft slippers (top) provided, oddly, by Air New Zealand), met some of its monks (left) and saw, of all things, a 7th century lavatory, celebrated as much for its ornate decoration as for its age. Prince Philip refused to give a demonstration and was in jocular mood when he said of a 40-foot-high statue of Buddha: "That's a very, very big Buddha."

A 100-mile car journey to Kandy followed. It took the Queen and

OCTOBER 1981

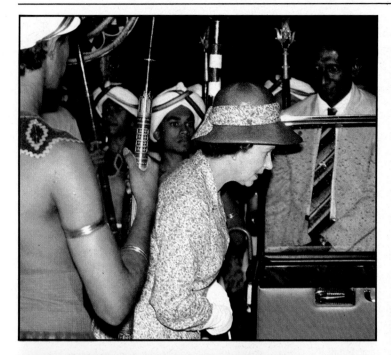

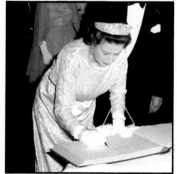

Prince Philip through miles of exotic spice forests which looked the more dramatic when heavy rain fell as a reminder of the monsoon period. The roads were winding and mountainous, crowds, huddled under colourful umbrellas, stood waiting at every village, and elephants toiled in plantations as the royal party passed. Massive decorative wickerwork archways welcomed their arrival in Kandy where a civic reception awaited them (top right). Here the Queen was presented with a sword-fruit flower brooch, set with blue sapphires, rubies and diamonds, and a navaratne – a jewel consisting of nine gems, said to ward off the ill effects of planetary activity. Both she and Prince Philip were led back to their car beneath huge ceremonial umbrellas (right and far left), to prepare for the evening's luxuriant State banquet.

Immediately prior to this scintillating event was a *perahera* – a glittering torchlight procession of bands, dancers and elephants all in full carnival swing (this page). Despite drizzling weather, Kandy was assembled to a man, and all was

en fête as, right into the early hours of the next morning, elephants, twinkling with coloured lights run from batteries mounted on their heads, were marched up and down the streets to the crack of whips and pistol shots. Daredevil jugglers tossed firebrands into the air, and dancers whirled and gyrated to the entrancing beat of drums and wail of pipes.

The Queen, wearing a dazzling white silk evening dress, watched it all from a pagoda-style building before she attended the banquet. She could

not contain her gratitude to her hosts and she said so in her speech: "I want to say how especially touched Prince Philip and I have been by the wonderful, friendly crowds who have greeted us. It has been a very moving experience." Neither could she resist connecting her visit with history. "As we come here tonight, to this beautiful old house," she continued, "I am reminded how the histories of our people have been intertwined over the centuries. This house was the residence of a long line of British Governors and also of Lord

Mountbatten."

The civilities were returned by the Queen when she gave a dinner for her hosts at the Lanka Oberoi Hotel (see page 44, left centre and bottom right) on the following evening, 24th October. This occasion ended the last full day's engagements which were fortunately not as tiring as those of 23rd.

At Pogolla, not far from Kandy, the Queen saw the building of the massive Victoria Dam which, when completed in 1984, will harness Sri Lanka's largest river, the Mahabelli, to provide a comprehensive and vital irrigation scheme and urban water supply. The project has

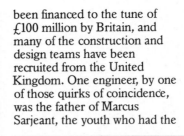

been financed to the tune of £100 million by Britain, and many of the construction and design teams have been recruited from the United Kingdom. One engineer, by one of those quirks of coincidence, was the father of Marcus Sarjeant, the youth who had the

massive cables carrying buckets of materials overhead linked one hill with another.

After watching a display of singing and dancing by children of the British community there, the Queen and Prince Philip visited Peradeniya where Sri Lanka's most exotic botanical

previous month been jailed for firing blank shots at the Queen in June. He decided to stay away from the official ceremonies to avoid causing embarrassment. Villagers had trekked from miles around to give the Queen and Prince Philip a rousing welcome at Victoria and the reservoir at the foot of the hills gleamed like a jewel as the Queen unveiled an obelisk to commemorate her visit, and looked down from a railed pavilion onto the project below. The royal couple then drove up to the hills to see other parts of the scheme in progress, which the Queen photographed avidly with her camera, as

gardens are. The area was once the site of the palace of the King of Kandy and the highly decorative gates evidence its tribal, royal past. The profusion of exotic plants and trees made the Chelsea Flower Show something of a runner-up – there were blooms of every size and colour, from the most delicate and subtle to the most gaudy and massive.

The Duke of Edinburgh was invited to plant an Asoka tree, one which is native to Sri Lanka and bears large clusters of heavily-scented flowers which change from yellow to flame-red. He performed this task rather perfunctorily, dropping the sapling into the hole provided, shovelling a couple of spadefuls of earth into it and dousing the finished result with a liberal sprinkling of water from a gold-coloured watering-can. The Queen, meanwhile, was being shown round the gardens, escorted by military guards

her arrival had been. A similar huge Guard of Honour to be inspected (opposite page, left), full honours with the playing of National Anthems (below and opposite page, top right) and the full complement of ministerial dignitaries, including the President and his wife (below left). As the Queen waved her last farewell (bottom centre) the rolling up of the red carpet (opposite page, top) confirmed the end of a most splendid visit.

The previous night, the Queen had said she was "absolutely delighted" by her visit. It was no less than Sri Lanka's own reaction. The national radio called it "a superbly successful visit," the Mint struck a new 2-rupee coin to commemorate it and the Ceylon Daily News' 64-page colour supplement was hopelessly oversubscribed.

resplendent in their red tunics and holding those great ceremonial umbrellas above her head. She had already planted a tree – the Gotu Nuga – here in 1954, and today her presence was commemorated by the naming of a rare orchid after her – dendrobium Elizabetha Regina II. She was presented with two specimens of the strain – a hybrid of complex parentage which produces long, upright bursts of blooms – one for herself and one for the Princess of Wales.

The Queen's departure at noon on 25th October was almost as spectacular and well-attended as

OCTOBER 1981

One of the most tactful and well-received royal decisions of 1981 was that the Prince and Princess of Wales would begin their public life's work together with a three-day visit to Wales itself. After a prolonged holiday at Balmoral, during which the only public engagement they undertook was the traditional royal attendance at the Braemar Gathering early in September, it seemed not only desirable but also a natural consequence of

Castle (left and below far left), where Prince Charles was ceremonially invested as Prince of Wales in July 1969. Here they were met formally – and informally (below and below left) by Lord Snowdon as Constable of the Castle. After spending an hour there, they were off to Bangor and Plas

their position and title that they should choose the Principality as the venue of their first public engagements.

Their schedule was one of the sort normally associated with State visits; eleven or twelve hours each day, excluding travelling time to the first engagement and from the last. Lunch never exceeded an hour. With eighteen towns to visit it was very much a whistle-stop tour, reminiscent of Gladstone's election campaigns.

On 27th October the Prince and Princess paid visits to Deeside Leisure Centre (above) and Shotton, Rhyl and Caernarfon

Newydd, rounding off a day which surprised even the Press with its popular enthusiasm. Wind of North Wales' reception prompted the people of the south-west of the Principality to turn out in vast numbers the following day. They watched the royal couple visit St David's Cathedral (opposite page,

bottom left) for a service which revealed that the Princess had not yet learned very much Welsh, and they stood in pouring rain to greet them at Haverfordwest, Carmarthen and Llandeilo. A superb gala concert at Swansea, after which the Princess was surrounded by youngsters offering gifts (bottom

left and centre), completed a hectic second day.

The final day, 29th October, brought the tour to the South where the public response was at its wildest. The day began with the opening of the Young Farmers' Club at the Royal Welsh Showground at Llanelwedd (far left) and there were subsequent walkabouts in Pontypridd (left) and Brecon (below and bottom). During a

visit to Llwynypia Hospital the Prince and Princess inspected the maternity wing and Prince Charles spoke of the benefits of fathers seeing their children born. His words hit the next day's papers, though no-one suspected the news of the Princess' own pregnancy, which was announced to a delighted nation the following week.

NOVEMBER 1981

Almost the entire Royal Family paid their annual visit to the Royal Albert Hall to attend the Royal British Legion's Festival of Remembrance on 7th November. Among the less senior members were the Duchess of Kent (below, far right) and her sister-in-law Princess Michael (below centre) – both of whom in their choice of dress combined the subtle

blend of remembrance and festivity that makes the occasion both poignant and enjoyable. The Prime Minister and her husband (above) were amongst the distinguished non-royal guests, while the Queen and Prince Philip (top right) were of course the last of all to arrive. With them were the Prince of Wales and for the first time the Princess (top), only two days after announcing the expected birth of her first child. The Festival was also attended by the Queen Mother, the Duke and Duchess of Gloucester and Princess Alice, and by Prince

Andrew, who could little have suspected that within a few months he would be in the centre of the theatre of another war whose dead would be commemorated at the next Festival.

The programme took its familiar course. First, the muster of representatives from all armed forces and auxiliary services, each group led by its standard bearer as it made its way from the back of the Hall to the massive stage. Then the demonstrations, aimed at showing the great variety of support services in action – first aid, signalling, medical rehabilitation, preparations for battle. Then the gymnastic displays and the community singing, culminating in the short solemn service of remembrance led by the Bishop of London. Finally the fall of poppies – each

poppy representing a life lost in battle since the beginning of World War I. The Festival was concluded by the singing of the National Anthem and the raising of three cheers for Her Majesty. On the following morning the Royal Family were at Whitehall to participate in the Remembrance Day Service. It was another "first" for the Princess of Wales, who saw her husband, in the uniform of a Commander in the Royal Navy, lay a wreath on the Cenotaph (far right) after the Queen (right) and Prince Philip. The Duke of Kent also laid a wreath, and as usual the Queen Mother's was placed on her behalf by Major Sir Ralph Anstruther, while she watched from the Home Office balcony accompanied by Princess Alice

Duchess of Gloucester, the Princess of Wales and King Olav V of Norway who, like his father before him, always comes to London especially for the service.

Like the annual gift of a Norwegian-grown Christmas tree for London's Trafalgar Square, King Olav's presence from year to year is an expression of Norway's gratitude for Britain's stand against Nazi Germany during the early years of the War, and for the welcome Britain gave to King Haakon VII and the then Crown Prince Olav when they escaped from Norway in 1940 to head a provisional

government in London. The Remembrance Day Service, which changes little each year, was memorable for the presence of the Leader of the Opposition, who attended in a green donkey jacket and baggy trousers, exhibiting a demeanour which many found undignified. Surrounding ranks of spruce, black coats did indeed make him look out of place, though in the resulting furore, one newspaper reader thought even this preferable to the military dress adopted by a large number of those present, which tended to glorify or romanticise war.

DECEMBER 1981

On 11th December 1981, Prince Charles visited *HMS Osprey* at the Royal Naval Air School, Portland, Dorset, to present Observers Wings to members of 97 Maritime Helicopter Course. He may well have been thinking of that day, seven years less a day before, when he himself passed out as a fully qualified pilot at the Royal Naval Air School at Yeovilton.

It is no secret that the Royal Family's links with the Navy are as old as the Navy itself and that Prince Charles can trace several lines in his own family – his father, grandfather and great grandfather; the Mountbattens; Prince Alfred, Duke of Edinburgh; Queen Victoria's father; and King William IV – which illustrate the great fascination in which the Navy has held its members. Prince Louis of Battenberg, without whose "interest and enthusiasm," as Prince Charles once acknowledged, "the Naval Air Service might quite literally have had great difficulty in getting off the ground," helped to found the Service at the beginning of the First World War. Twenty years earlier he told the future King George V that "there is no more fitting preparation for a King than to have been trained in the Navy," and Prince Louis' son, Lord Mountbatten, said as much

again to King George VI forty-four years later. The message clearly got through to Prince Charles.

His spell at the Royal Naval Air School at Yeovilton lasted for the three months between September and December 1974, accounting for only five per cent of his five-year naval career. His initiation into the Navy may be said to have occurred when, as a member of the Gordonstoun School Cadet Force, he took part in sea training with the Royal Navy at Portsmouth in 1965. But his career proper did not start until just before his 23rd birthday, when he joined *HMS Norfolk* as a Sub-Lieutenant, following a six-week course at the Royal Naval College, Dartmouth. After service aboard *HMS Dryad* and *HMS Glasserton,* he joined the frigate *HMS Minerva* for a nine-month sailing, primarily in the West Indies, and it was during this time that he gained promotion to Acting Lieutenant. In January 1974 he joined another frigate *HMS Jupiter,* for an eight-month spell of service in the Far East, in which he served as a Communications Officer. It was on his return that he prepared for helicopter training at Yeovilton.

Like his father, Prince Philip, before him, he wanted to gain his helicopter wings to add to

the RAF wings he had already achieved after his six months at RAF College Cranwell, Lincolnshire, in 1971. But the Yeovilton course was not nearly as leisurely as Cranwell. Prince Charles found that his official engagements took him away from Yeovilton several times and his training time had to be concentrated into some 45 days only. In that time he had to complete at least fifty hours of training on the ground, a further forty hours flying in dual-controlled aircraft, and fifteen hours solo flying. In the event he flew solo for a total of 26 hours and thus more than earned his licence: no mean achievement since apart from the constant interruption caused by his royal

his Wessex V helicopter, or allied computer seizures, caused him to negotiate three emergency landings during those hectic 45 days. At best it gave him the chance to prove himself to himself and to the public. It may also have helped him gain the Double Diamond award for the trainee who showed the greatest rate and degree of progress throughout the course. Certainly his entire experience at the Royal Naval Air School endowed him with more than an honorary interest in the activities of *HMS Osprey*, whose crew's initiation came to a satisfactory conclusion in December 1981, and with the know-how which made his visit, with its inspection of the helicopters that would soon play

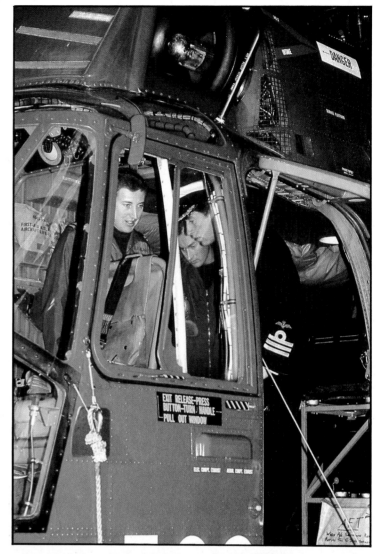

duties, he underwent a short but gruelling commando course at the Royal Marine School at Lympstone – a course he described as "very exciting, very rewarding, very stimulating, and sometimes bloody terrifying." The Yeovilton training provided no mere theoretical blooding: various failures in the engine of

a vital part in the recapture of the Falklands Islands, interesting and rewarding.
The visit may have rubbed in the unpalatable truth that pressure of royal business in the late 1970's prevented him from continuing with what he had discovered was his forte. When, on leaving his squadron, he

expressed the hope of being able to maintain his expertise, he must have known that it would be impossible. Safety considerations towards the heir made it so from the start although, as he himself said, "if you're living dangerously, it tends to make you appreciate your life that much more, and to

really want to live it to its fullest." But he has not lost touch. More often than not he pilots his own planes and helicopters around the country on official visits – and he even did so when leaving Eastleigh airport for Gibraltar on the first stage of his honeymoon!

DECEMBER 1981

The Queen, wearing a deep blue evening dress with a classic ornamental design in gold lamé, attended a Christmas carol recital at Fishmongers Hall in the City of London on 16th December. Accompanied by the Duke of Edinburgh she was welcomed by Sir Christopher Leaver (below) who had only the week before replaced Sir Ronald Gardner-Thorpe as Lord Mayor of London, and was also introduced to officials of the British Sailors' Society in aid of December of a final address from both Houses of the Canadian Parliament asking for the transfer of full constitutional power from Westminster to Canada – a request which portended the Queen's hastily-arranged visit to Ottawa the following April – and the courtesy call the next day from the colourful and unpredictable President Mobutu of Zaire, in London on a 2-day working visit. December brought a couple of surprises for the Queen – one of

which the concert was staged. The recital was one of only two official engagements undertaken by the Queen in public in December – the other, a week previously, was also in the City and involved a visit to the Baltic Exchange. But the Queen was not short of work that month, as she faced a heavy and varied programme of duties before escaping to Windsor for Christmas with the family. Most of those duties took place inside Buckingham Palace; few days went by without a series of audiences with incoming or retiring diplomats presenting Letters of Credence or Recall from their respective governments, and there was the monthly Palace Luncheon on 15th December when the guests, ranging from Osian Ellis the harpist to the Deputy Director General of the Prison Service, reflected in the usual way the diverse elements of the national way of life. Two particularly significant duties will have made themselves memorable however: the presentation on 9th

which was the spontaneous burst of applause given to her by the 80-strong congregation as she entered St Peter's Church Edensor for Mattins, during her weekend stay with the Duke of Devonshire at Chatsworth on 5th/6th December. The other, a week later, was her unexpected seven-hour stay at the Cross Hands Inn, Old Sodbury, after her Range Rover stuck in heavy snow as she was travelling from Gatcombe Park where she had been visiting Princess Anne. During December the Queen recorded her annual national and Commonwealth Christmas broadcast for television and radio. Its theme reflected 1981's most dedicated charity drive, the International Year of Disabled People, and the Queen's own words, spoken as usual from inside Buckingham Palace, were interspersed with film of a delightfully informal ceremony

which had taken place during the summer in the Palace grounds.

The film showed the Queen, the Duke of Edinburgh and the Prince and Princess of Wales handing over to disabled drivers sets of keys for motor cars specially designed to overcome their major physical handicaps. It says a lot for the Princess of Wales that in this, her first year as a public figure she should have appeared in the Royal Christmas Broadcast. King George V, who inaugurated the Christmas message by radio in 1932 and who was bowled over by his daughters-in-law and granddaughters, would have been charmed by his great-granddaughter's performance.

DECEMBER 1981

At eighty years of age Princess Alice, Duchess of Gloucester, has every intention of reducing the number of engagements she accepts. Easier said than done: "The trouble is that when you have been associated with organisations for many years and someone pleads with you to do

something you did for them last year, or they say it's all going to be a terrible flop if you don't go, what can you do?" Her staff see it differently, marvelling as she finds excuses to do things which a less resolute octogenarian would happily dodge.

She is probably as unconvinced of her age as anyone meeting her would be. A lively mind, a deceptive sense of humour and a phenomenal memory belie her eighty years every bit as much as her impeccable deportment and the straight back which, though her figure is much more petite, recall her mother-in-law Queen Mary.

Her memory goes back to the age of two or three, but, she warned "the story is too silly to relate." She remembers her sheer terror when, while being bathed one evening, the nursery door burst open. In tumbled two elder brothers, full of mischief, and a great boot landed "with a terrible splash" into the bathtub! A more embarrassing incident

befell when she and a younger sister were to present a single bouquet of flowers – "a fatal thing to arrange" – to Princess Louise, Duchess of Argyll when she opened the Hydropathic Institution at Melrose. At the last moment her sister suddenly shouted "I don't like *her*," snatched the bouquet away and presented it to someone else. Lady Alice Montagu-Douglas-Scott's childhood was typical of

the Edwardian aristocracy: governesses, nannies and the constant shifting between her father's three residences. Her mother was reserved and, it seems, rather a distant figure: her father, Duke of Buccleuch, an MP and Lord Lieutenant, was busy, little seen by his children, and immensely authoritarian. Even in her twenties he refused her an allowance for her to go to East Africa, so she held an exhibition of her paintings and used the proceeds for the trip. They were exciting days; she took photographs of wildlife which won prizes when she got back home.

Life changed considerably after she married the Duke of Gloucester, King George V's third son, in 1935. They were quietly devoted to each other and she was warmly welcomed into the family. The King, then a very sick man, was "very kind to me," and Queen Mary used to invite her over to Marlborough House of an evening when the

Duke was away. King George VI kindly wrote to her in 1942, when the Duke was abroad, "Do let me know when you want to come and stay at Windsor.

Her public life took her to most parts of the world, but Barnwell, her country home in Northamptonshire, is her haven. "Our weekends are very precious," she says, and these pictures of her with her three grandchildren (opposite page) say it all. She still shines on duty, as (opposite page top right) at Crosby Hall, a student residence in Chelsea, on 17th March, and was thrilled at

having her 80th birthday honoured by the presentation of a new rose, Blesma Soul, to her at Kensington Palace on 6th January (this page).

Her birthday fell on Christmas Day, when the entire Royal Family was at Windsor. Did she have a party? She checked a hollow laugh: "There's *always* a party. Princess Alexandra and I shared the cake!"

JANUARY 1982

One of the earliest royal engagements of 1982 was the visit by Prince and Princess Michael of Kent to St Paul's Cathedral to attend the Inaugural Celebration of the English Tourist Board's "Maritime England" Promotion. The promotion consists of over two thousand events which have and will continue to take place throughout England in 1982, from art exhibitions to sand castle competitions, regattas to concerts – all on a maritime theme.

The Inaugural Celebration was held on 14th January with a concert of music descriptive of, or connected with, the sea. Nine items made up the whole, with Mendelssohn's overture "Calm Sea and Prosperous Voyage," and the opening sequence from

Vaughan-Williams' "Sea Symphony" alternating with sea songs and naval miscellanies. It seemed that no expense was spared to give the event its initial lift: the Royal Philharmonic Orchestra was joined by the Band of the Royal Marines; the Bach Choir, with the Duchess of Kent as one of its members, performed as well, as did the Fanfare Trumpeters and Corps of Drums, who had previously performed at the Prince of Wales' Wedding in July. The Master of Ceremonies for the evening was BBC TV's newsreader and music lover Richard Baker.

"The Michaels," as Prince and Princess Michael are informally known, gave the concert that air of royal informality which creates enjoyment out of any imposing occasion. The Czech-born Princess, formerly Baroness von Reibnitz, sported one of her favourite lines in headgear, a petite, bowler-style veiled hat, while her husband was able to show off a beard of more luxuriant growth than ever before. It is the second time he has grown a beard since his marriage; this most recent attempt began in August and first came to public notice when he and Princess Michael went to Belize in September, on behalf of the Queen, to preside over the gaining of independence from Britain. Rarely is an opportunity missed to comment on how like he is to his grandfather King George V, but in an age when few royal princes grow beards, everything is relative. Perhaps it depends

upon what light you catch him in.

Prince Michael has now quit active service in the Army – he retired from the Royal Hussars with the rank of Major in March 1981. He has, however, obtained permission from the Queen to continue to wear uniform, and did so for the Royal Wedding the following July. He now has more time to spend attending official functions: indeed during 1981 he and his wife clocked up no fewer than 120. These were mostly in London as their expenses have to be met from their own private funds. Since Prince Michael's renunciation of his claim to the Throne (enforced by the operation of the Act of Settlement after his marriage to the Princess who is a Roman Catholic), he has not

within the Church of England and their places in the line of succession are assured. It is however unlikely that they will be called upon to perform official duties, since the Kent family is already well represented by the Duke of Kent and his two sons. In addition of course, as the Queen's own children produce families who will ultimately take up the more important royal duties, the pressure will be lifted from both the Gloucesters and the Kents who, representing King George V's younger sons, have been sharing the royal round with the

been entitled to receive any Civil List payments – nor do his and his wife's attendances at official functions warrant a mention in the Court Circular.

Prince and Princess Michael's two children, Lord Frederick Windsor, born in April 1979, and Lady Gabriella, born in April 1981, are both being brought up

Queen and her more immediate family. By then both Lord Frederick and Lady Gabriella, now 19th and 20th respectively in the line of succession, will have been pushed so far down as to make it only academically possible for them to succeed to the Throne.

(Centre left) On 19th January Princess Alexandra paid a visit to Alexandra House at Bromley in Kent, the headquarters of the Cystic Fibrosis Research Trust of which she is Patron. On 17th February (left and below left) she was escorted round the exhibition "Excavating in Egypt" which opened that day at the British Museum. The exhibition, mounted to celebrate the centenary of the Egypt Exploration Society, did not include a small section of the Sphinx's beard which the Egyptian authorities have for some time been hoping to retrieve from the British Museum's custody and restore to its rightful place on the Sphinx at the foot of the Giza pyramids.

(Opposite page) Princess Alexandra in animated mood when she attended a fashion show at the Japanese Embassy Residence in London on 25th January. The show, presented by designer Hanai Mori, was staged in aid of the Mental Health Foundation of which the Princess is Patron. She and her husband, the Hon Angus Ogilvy, were treated to a long succession of vivid and elegant designs, drawn from many different national cultures and betraying influences of fashions past and present (right).

The Princess' 1982 engagements began somewhat earlier than those of most members of the Royal Family, and January was a comparatively busy month.

JANUARY 1982

Penlee is one of those names which, unknown to 99% of Britain's population for generations, suddenly becomes a household word for decades. It is to the history of the sea what Lewisham and Harrow are to the railways, Aberfan to the coal industry, Flixborough to the chemical industry. On 19th December 1981, in the grip of one of the iciest autumns for years, a coaster, the *Union Star,* listing helplessly in mountainous seas, tried in vain to reach shelter on the South Cornish coast. In an attempt to save the eight people on board, the Penlee lifeboat *Solomon Browne* set out in impossible weather and amid a confusion of signals from the distressed ship. Her mission was doomed: the lifeboat was pushed remorselessly towards the rocks where in

men to their deaths. The church, which overlooks the stricken village, had three of the dead crew buried in its churchyard, and the RNLI flag fluttered noisily at half mast as the Duke and Duchess arrived to be greeted by a guard of honour made up of 25 lifeboatmen, some of them related to the victims of the disaster. Inside were five hundred local people, crammed in as nothing before witnessed there. A further 200 people huddled together in a marquee to which the service was relayed. RNLI branches throughout Britain had requested places for representatives, but had to be told that the service was strictly limited to local interest and that room for wider public condolence would be available at a memorial service to be held at Truro

heaving seas she was smashed to pieces. Eight of her volunteer crew died, and in that one terrible venture five women were widowed and a dozen children rendered fatherless.

In the wake of the immediate tragedy, help came from all parts of the country. Even before an enquiry could get under way a voluntary fund was set up and thousands of pounds poured in to help the bereaved families and set the tiny village community back on its feet again. On 22nd January, the 81st anniversary of one death – that of Queen Victoria – which unleashed national grief of a different kind, the Duke of Kent, as President of the Royal National Lifeboat Institution, and the Duchess of Kent, attended a Family Service of Remembrance and Thanksgiving in the Parish Church in Mousehole.

It was a sharp, windswept day, but the skies were blue and little indication existed of the monstrous conditions which only a month before had sent

Cathedral the following month. The service lasted barely three quarters of an hour, and was very simple. The Duke of Kent read the lesson and a local television personality, Mr Clive Gunnell, gave an address praising selflessness and preferring the regenerative spirit to the cold stone memorial. When it was all over the Duke and Duchess, accompanied by

the Vicar, the Reverend Hugh Cadman, went to the vicarage to meet the bereaved families privately. The Duchess, clutching a wrapped bunch of flowers presented to her there, assured them that her sympathy was with them all. "I hope this is a day you will never forget, but also a day that will never come again," she said. To Mrs Mary Greenhalgh, whose husband's death had left her as licensee of the Ship Inn, the Duchess made the promise that when she was next in Cornwall on holiday she would come to her pub and have a drink. Both the Duke and the Duchess gave full rein to the only sentiment they could possibly contribute. "They were very sympathetic and expressed the hope that we would be able to pick up the threads of our lives," said one woman. The Duke was poignantly impressed. "It was a deeply moving service," he said. "It was magnificent to meet the families. They showed so much courage

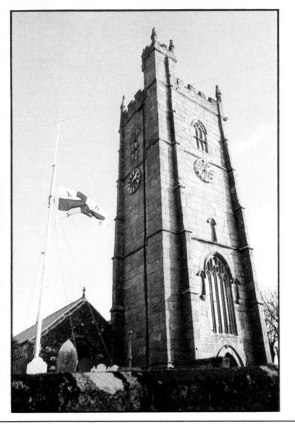

and were such a great inspiration."

Since the 22nd January the courage has continued. The funds have poured in from all parts of the country and beyond its shores. A new contingent of men from Penlee and Mousehole have offered themselves as replacements for their lost neighbours in the unending and invaluable service of the RNLI. Slowly, and not without the distress which fundamental readjustment in the full glare of publicity invariably brings, life has begun to assume something approaching normality. But the personal tragedy lives on, with a severity which blights each succeeding birthday, wedding anniversary and Christmas celebration with its persistent reminder that a loved one is irretrievably absent. Long after other national and international calamities have

overwhelmed the horror of Penlee, its widows and orphans will grieve privately at last. But they will be touched by the memory of the visit of the Duke and Duchess of Kent in the hour when the need for consolation and moral support was greatest. For one afternoon this short but heartfelt royal visit brought the nation's attention to the plight of one of its smallest villages, bereft of a proportion of its manhood which in a major city would have been regarded as a national disaster. Here and now the disaster existed only within the heart of a tiny community where no-one remained unaffected by the reality of what lifeboatmen the world over regard as an occupational hazard.

FEBRUARY 1982

On 2nd February Queen Elizabeth the Queen Mother undertook her second public engagement of 1982 when she visited Canada House to open its new Cultural Centre. After her arrival she was taken up to the High Commissioner's Office for a short private meeting. A quarter of an hour later she came down the stairs (below) escorted by the High Commissioner Mrs Jean Casselman Wadds (below right) and led by a piper – Lieutenant Mike Ward of the Royal Canadian Dragoons. Once into the auditorium at the foot of the stairs, she declared the Cultural Centre open and received a vote of thanks from the Canadian Minister of Culture and Public Affairs, Mr John Graham.

The ceremony was short but it kept alive the Queen Mother's links with Canada which were forged almost forty-three years before. In 1939, less than three years after their accession, she accompanied King George VI on an exhausting and comprehensive 6-week State Visit there, which took them from coast to coast, and eclipsed even the brilliant State Visit to France the previous year. It was nearly written off when their ship *Empress of Australia* almost hit an iceberg at about the spot where *HMS Titanic* foundered in 1912, and almost on the anniversary of the tragedy. But the royal arrival at Quebec on 17th May 1939 made King George VI the first reigning British sovereign to tread on the soil of what was then fondly known as British North America. The tour was a resounding success. Travel was mostly by

the "silver and blue train" as it was familiarly known – a 300-ton blue and aluminium CPR locomotive pulling twelve streamlined coaches over a total of more than 9,000 miles in the course of the six-week tour from Quebec to Vancouver and back to Halifax. At every station – and with a full programme which left very little time for relaxation there were many stations – there was a crowd to greet the King and Queen. Like most tours this one had its formal and informal moments. For the Queen, the laying of the foundation stone for the new Supreme Court building in Ottawa was perhaps the most memorable. She mused on the fact that she, and not the King, had been asked to lay the stone,

but concluded that the choice was appropriate as "woman's position in modern society has depended upon the growth of law." Amongst the more informal interludes was the private visit to see the famous Dionne quins who had been born in Canada six years earlier. The Queen herself was credited with miraculous powers when, despite persistent rain during a drive through Winnipeg, she instructed that the car's roof should be let down so that people could see her. Almost immediately the rain stopped! But she seemed to have enough personal magic of her own. As one commentator said, "As for the Queen she appeared and the day was won. So simple in her bearing and yet so refined, so spontaneous in every move and yet so harmonious; so radiant with feminine charm and so expressive of emotion, she also found the true words for every occasion and every person." The Queen enjoyed the tour too. "It made us," she confided to the Canadian Prime Minister Mr Mackenzie King.

The tour was almost as famous for the few days the King and Queen spent in the United States, where they were the guests of President Franklin Roosevelt and his accomplished wife Eleanor. The President's informal style was much appreciated by his guest, the modest, retiring King, and their personal letters to each other – "My dear President Roosevelt," "My dear King George" – reflected the kindred spirits. Perhaps the most informal incident of the trip came when, after a private evening dinner and a long talk, the President suddenly said to the King: "Well, young man, it's time for you to go to bed!"

Apart from the great personal success the King and Queen scored with the President, the triumphant reception accorded to them by the people of New York and the Atlantic seaboard surpassed all precedents. George III's descendant and his wife conquered the old colonies at the first attempt!

None of the Queen Mother's subsequent visits to Canada ever equalled the scale and sparkle of the 1939 tour. But in 1954 she was back again, spending five days in Ottawa. Because of her visit she was unable to be in

London for Prince Charles' sixth birthday, but he was thrilled to receive a transatlantic telephone call from her instead. In June 1962 she went to Montreal to attend the centenary celebrations of the Black Watch (Royal Highland Regiment) of Canada, of which she is Colonel-in-Chief, and three years later celebrated the jubilee of the Toronto Scottish Regiment.

A slightly more prolonged visit was arranged in July 1967 when a 10-day programme took her to

the Atlantic provinces of New Brunswick, Nova Scotia, Prince Edward Island and Newfoundland. In June 1974 she was back again to present new Colours to each of her two regiments in Toronto and Montreal. Three years ago she paid a seven-day visit to Halifax and Toronto and in July 1981 attended the bicentennial celebrations of Niagara on the Lake during another 7-day visit to Ontario.

Four days after she opened the Cultural Centre at Canada House, the thirtieth anniversary of her widowhood came round. Her seven visits to Canada in those 30 years and the Canadian connections she nurtures in Britain have maintained the commitment engendered by that first great tour when she herself said, "When I'm in Canada, I am a Canadian."

FEBRUARY 1982

To the Queen and the Duke of Edinburgh, Buckingham Palace probably seemed a much emptier place in 1982 than it had ever been since the beginning of the Queen's reign. The Prince of Wales' wedding in July 1981 (right, with the Princess of Wales on honeymoon at Balmoral in August) and the newly-weds' subsequent removal to Highgrove in November and Kensington Palace in June deprived the old home of the heir to the Throne's constant presence. With Prince Andrew out in the South Atlantic and Prince Edward due to go to New Zealand in the autumn, the Queen and Prince Philip faced the unusual prospect of playing Darby and Joan for the first time.

Prince Andrew (below) who has already gained his wings, continued his final operational

training as a Sea King pilot in 1981 with an unexpected flourish when he was involved in a real life rescue of a sailor swept overboard from the submarine *HMS Ocelot* in the Firth of Clyde in September. Prince Andrew was at the controls of his helicopter when the accident happened and was able to manoeuvre the Sea King until it hovered above the scene sufficiently long for the sailor to be rescued. Even more unexpected was his journey to the South Atlantic on board *HMS Invincible* in April at the beginning of what was to be a ten-week combined services operation to recapture the Falkland Islands.

Meanwhile, Prince Edward (top right) celebrated his eighteenth birthday on 10 March 1982 working out his

penultimate term at Gordonstoun, confident in the knowledge that his coming of age had brought him the present of over £16,000 a year from the Civil List. He has now passed his 'A' levels in English, History and Economics, following which he took a post as junior master and house tutor at Collegiate School, Wanganui, on the North Island of New Zealand, in September. The school is the second oldest in New Zealand

and boasts a complement of 545 boys, for each of whom the school receives fees of £2,000 per year. The school is a highly conformist one, relying on "disciplined learning, manners, dress, bearing and chapel worship" and the headmaster, Mr Ian McKinnon, was sure that Prince Edward would enjoy himself immensely. He will, spend two terms at Wanganui. The remaining photographs on these pages show the Queen and the Queen is not abroad at the time, the accession anniversary was spent as part of the last week or so of her New Year holiday at this well-loved private family residence, bought by the future King Edward VII over a century ago.

Out of respect for the Queen Mother, whose husband's death brought the Queen to the Throne on this day in 1952, the anniversary was not publicly celebrated except by the

Prince Philip at Sandringham, appearing before the cameras on 4th February for photographs released two days later, the thirtieth anniversary of the Queen's accession to the Throne. As in most years when traditional flying of flags on all public buildings, and the gun salutes at the Tower of London and in Hyde Park.

FEBRUARY 1982

Prince Philip became President of World Wildlife Fund International in May 1981 and in February 1982 began one of what may become a series of crash courses to familiarise himself with conservation problems in all parts of the world. In a three-week tour

which he was serenaded (bottom right) during lunch by a local violinist.

(Below) In New Delhi Prince Philip presented the keys of two jeeps to the Asian Elephant Group at the Maurya Sheraton Hotel, after he had watched two audio visual shows detailing some of the World Wildlife Fund's Indian operations. Earlier that day he met the Prime Minister, Mrs Indira Gandhi (opposite page) and had lunch with her.

Prince Philip's 36-hour visit to Oman, where he was the guest of the Sultan (who paid a State Visit to Britain the following month) was arranged primarily to enable him to see the progress of one of the most exciting of all World Wildlife

which began on 17th February and took him to countries as far apart as Spain and Sri Lanka, he witnessed a wide range of activities from the minting of commemorative medals in Vienna to the reintroduction of captive oryx into the deserts of Oman.

In Austria he visited a compound (top right) at Haringsee where wild birds, including this ferocious-looking bearded vulture (opposite page top), are reared for research purposes, and a bird sanctuary (above right) at Marchegg, near the Czechoslovakian border. He had earlier been taken on a waggon ride round the Seewinkel to tour extensive wetlands populated with geese and other marsh birds, after

Fund's hundreds of projects. A decade ago the Arabian white oryx was almost extinct in the wild, a victim, like so many other species, of the trade in horn. The last few were rounded up and reared in a long-term programme of captivity and have only just been released back into the wild. The Duke arrived at the desert base at Yalooni, a two-hour helicopter journey from Muscat, to see how the oryx's reintroduction was progressing.

On arrival he met Dr and Mrs Mark Stanley-Price who run the project (bottom left) and was taken by landrover to where the oryx could be seen.

Unfortunately the previous night had brought a 1½″ rainfall, the first rain for 5 years, and some of the Duke's wanderings on foot became a little hazardous (left). But he was able to see ten pure white oryx grazing placidly among acacia, eronbergiana and prosopis trees, and the project staff were particularly proud that one of the oryx had produced a healthy calf, now nine months old, which was adapting as well as the adults to its new environment. The Duke was fascinated to meet the local Bedou tribesmen (far left) who, armed with rifles, now have the job of protecting the herd from poachers.

On 7th March Prince Philip's tour took him to Port Sudan where the Sudanese Navy was

waiting to take him and World Wildlife Fund officials to a coral reef some twenty miles out to sea. The expedition had the advantage of the best weather of the tour, though the swell during the outward journey kept a few of the passengers fairly subdued. Even the Duke was on the point of succumbing towards the end, and on disembarking opted to climb the lighthouse *before* taking lunch! From the top of the lighthouse – "257 steps, if you're interested," he said on the way down – the brilliant variations in the sea's colour could be seen, while a walk along the jetty brought the sight

FEBRUARY 1982

During his two-day visit to India, Prince Philip travelled from Jaipur to visit a tiger reserve at Sariska, about 150 miles south of New Delhi. On his arrival at the reserve headquarters tea was served in the garden and the layout of the reserve was explained (opposite page, bottom right) with details of the forty or so species of animals and birds which are known to inhabit it. A three-jeep convoy then left (centre pictures) for a fascinating two-hour journey deep into the reserve. There was

no risk of being met by tigers, which come out only at night, but a large variety of wildlife was in evidence. Deer, neatly camouflaged in the dense woodland, were betrayed by shafts of sunlight filtering through, but showed little sign of nervousness as the jeeps slowed to allow their passengers a glimpse. The occasional jackal was spotted, blue-bull and rhesus monkeys abounded, the nests of weaver-birds dangled and swung from tall trees, and buzzards drifted high against

of brightly coloured fish, crabs and shoals of sardinellos in the rocky shallows (right). Prince Philip was taken by boat to look for fish in the deeper waters (above right) before returning to Port Sudan (centre and top left). From there he went to Suakin – almost a ghost town now since it literally fell to pieces thirty years ago or so – to record his visit to a small research centre (opposite page, bottom left).

lofty crags. On the way back the Duke stopped at a look-out post from which tourists (who were not admitted on this day) can watch for tigers – but although that part of the visit was extended into the early hours of dusk, no tiger was sighted. On the return journey the stench of rotting meat heralded the quite gripping spectacle of a score of buzzards tearing at the corpse of some unfortunate animal, and flaunting grisly morsels of dripping flesh in savage beaks. For this is no animal sanctuary,

is a problem the Germans will have to sort out for themselves. I am sure you can find a compromise on this."
He went to Sri Lanka to see the operation of a massive project which involves the reorganisation of whole communities of elephants with human populations and industrial complexes to provide the most efficient interplay between the multiple needs of each. He visited Sri Lanka's two biggest sanctuaries – at Yale and Wilpattu – and during a visit to

into the Parque Donana, a huge – indeed Europe's largest – wetland wildlife preserve, where he spent most of the afternoon and evening being driven from habitat to habitat.
In Madrid there was a meeting with his cousin King Juan Carlos of Spain; and the affectionate welcome given to him by Queen Sophie made it obvious that despite the fracas over the Royal Wedding, the personal relationships between the English and Spanish royal families were as strong as ever.

except in that it is protected from the ravages of man. The cruelties of nature – as man might see it – are allowed their course in the interests of the delicate balance of life in the wild, and the fact was uncompromisingly illustrated by this chance encounter with the stark reality.
The Duke's tour also took him to Egypt, where poor weather unfortunately put paid to a visit to an oasis in the Sinai and

limited his activities to a view of the Giza Pyramids and, as he somewhat bitterly put it, "a look at Cairo's traffic."
An earlier leg of the tour found the Duke in the midst of a controversy in the province of Schleswig-Holstein, in northern Germany. Here the government is proposing to build a six-mile dyke across a nature reserve of 8400 acres, and ecologists are convinced that the project will threaten the natural uses to which this marshland is put. Hundreds of thousands of migratory birds use it, millions of sea birds find it a convenient breeding ground, and it also houses shallow-living sea life like crabs and mussels.
The Duke had to tread gingerly between the interests of the administration, who were concerned to prevent the loss of life and property in the event of a severe flood, and the ecologists who feared the loss of wildlife amenities. He achieved his neutral stance with his usual accomplishment. Speaking in fluent German he said, "Both interests are perfectly valid. This

a zoo in Colombo, he was presented with a baby elephant, named Geetha, which is now in London Zoo.
He visited further projects in Italy and Tunisia and finished the entire tour with a 2-day visit to Spain. Here he visited the Gonzales Byass sherry bodegas before joining a field trip at Sanlucar de Barrameda near Jerez. He enjoyed an open air lunch before crossing the Rio Guadalquivir by navy launch

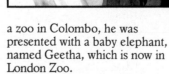

Prince Philip returned to Heathrow airport on 12th March at the end of his three week tour, during which it was announced that he had been appointed Vice-President of the International Union for the Conservation of Nature and Natural Resources – the scientific branch of the World Wildlife Fund.

FEBRUARY 1982

One of the most prestigious diplomatic events of February was the Ambassadorial Ball Soirée Française held on 22nd February at Grosvenor House in aid of the United Nations Association and UNICEF. This year's royal guest was the Duchess of Gloucester, sparkling as always in appearance and in form, seen (above and opposite page) as she arrived for the Soirée. The distinguished company included the patrons of honour – twenty five Ambassadors and High Commissioners – and another 25 patrons representing a vast range of national life – Margaret Duchess of Argyll and Lulu, Group-Captain Leonard Cheshire and Stirling Moss, Yehudi Menuhin and Esther Rantzen. Eric Morecambe, another patron, was there and the Duchess clearly enjoyed his company (top pictures). So much so that she may even have been tempted to appear in his next show!

The programme for the six-hour entertainment was superb. After the champagne reception, the guests were serenaded during a dinner of cream of cress soup, seafood pancake, suprème de volaille and cherries with praline ice cream. A fashion spectacular by the New Bond Street fashion house Ungaro followed, before Johnny Howard and his Orchestra led the dancing until the midnight cabaret. A couple of raffles were held, with holidays in Bali, India and Tunisia as prizes in one, and jewellery, clothes and wines contributing to a 13-part prize

list in the other. For those with energy to spare there was a discotheque until 2.00 in the morning.

The Duchess left somewhat earlier than that but even so was probably relieved that she had no engagements to fulfil the following day.

FEBRUARY 1982

Many of the Queen's visits to establishments in London happen because she is Patron of the host organisations, and they generally involve the perfunctory business of unveiling plaques and touring buildings. Thus, for instance, on 11th February, in her capacity as Patron of the British Institute of Radiology, she opened its new headquarters in Portland Place (right and below right), and again on 24th March, as Patron of the London Hospital, she opened the new Alexandra Wing at Whitechapel (below).

On each occasion yet another plaque was unveiled, to record, with due formality and sense of permanence, both a new chapter in the institution's history and

is a judge – known as the Queen's Remembrancer – presiding over a jury of twenty-four goldsmiths, both male and female, who inspect and assay the coinage to be laid out before them. After they have been duly sworn in, a procession of oak chests arrives (this is where the word Pyx comes in: it derives from the Greek word for "box"), and their contents are emptied into bowls of wood and bronze. At this year's Trial, those contents amounted to almost 35,000 coins in all, with a face value of £152,000. Most were United Kingdom coins, but a few were bound for New Zealand. Amongst the British coinage were over 2,600 sovereigns and thirty-four pieces

another in the interminable line of unveilings performed by the Queen since her public engagements began in 1946. And, to keep the royal Patron up-to-date with the latest developments in research and achievement, each building was duly toured, its staff introduced and its exhibitions inspected. There was something of a change on 25th February, when the Queen became the first monarch for almost four hundred years to attend the annual Trial of the Pyx at Goldsmiths Hall, London. Few of our many and varied national traditions go back to Saxon times, but the Trial of the Pyx is one that does.

It sounds whimsical enough to merit a mention in "Lord of the Rings" but in fact its purpose – even now more than merely ceremonial – is to test the size, appearance, weight and purity of samples of the gold, silver and cupro-nickel coins which have been produced by the Royal Mint at Llantrisant in mid-Glamorgan within the previous twelve months. To achieve this, many of the elements of a criminal trial are present. There

of Maundy money, which Her Majesty would be distributing at St David's Cathedral two months later.

The Queen's arrival (top right) at Goldsmiths Hall marked the beginning of the 700th Trial since King Edward I issued the first formal directive for the coinage to be comprehensively tested, in 1282. Official records have been fairly meticulously kept since then by the Librarian of Goldsmiths Hall – a position

currently held by Miss Susan Hare – but considerable doubt surrounds the question of the last monarch to attend the Trial. The written record shows that King James I was the last to pay his respects, and that no sovereign has attended since 1611. But the story goes that his grandson King Charles II put in an appearance in 1669: though the story carries little credibility, presumably on the grounds that the King was more preoccupied with quantities of cash than with its quality.

Whatever the truth of the matter, the Queen performed her long-overdue resurrection of yet another royal tradition with the perfection we have come almost to take for granted. With Sir Geoffrey Howe – Master of the Mint as well as Chancellor of the Exchequer – in tow, she duly sifted through the quantities of coins to be assayed. Please God it made a pleasant change from unveiling plaques.

The Queen Mother, whose official engagements these days tend to be understandably fewer than the Queen's, continued her public round with a visit to St Peter's Church, Walworth to attend a thanksgiving service

forged in unforgettable style at the 1937 Coronation. Then, Londoners gave her and King George VI a rapturous reception which served admirably as an antidote to the unsettling and embittering effect of the Abdication crisis five months previously. The relationship was strengthened in 1940 when she visited several areas of East London which had suffered badly – in terms of life and property – during the Blitz. Her oft-quoted statement, shortly after the first bombing of Buckingham Palace, that "I'm glad we've been bombed: it makes me feel I can look the East End in the face," was no banality: for some months before, East Londoners had

begun to lose heart so badly that even royal visits failed to placate a growing feeling of resentment towards the establishment.

The Queen Mother became Chancellor of London University in 1955 – a post she held with the utmost enthusiasm for a quarter of a century. Further ties with the capital followed her appointment as Patron of the London Gardens Society, in

there on the evening of 23rd February. This was a happy, informal and friendly occasion, as witness the effusive greeting Her Majesty received from the Dean (pictures far right) and the beaming smiles on her own face as well as on that of the Bishop of Southwark, Michael Marshall. He and the Queen Mother had a common link, be it ever so tenuous, in that he was educated at Lincoln School, to whose pastoral church, Lincoln Cathedral, the Queen Mother went as Duchess of York in 1932 to attend a thanksgiving service for its restoration.

The visit perpetuated the Queen Mother's special personal links with East and South London,

which capacity she still pays annual visits to the most beautiful of South and West London's domestic gardens. She has even played snooker during visits to Boys' Clubs in East London, and a recent visit to Smithfield Meat Market demonstrated that she has lost none of her old appeal with the true Cockney.

FEBRUARY 1982

On 27th February the Prince and Princess of Wales arrived at London's Heathrow Airport after a ten-day holiday in the Bahamas. They had been guests of Lord and Lady Romsey at Windermere, Countess Mountbatten's home on the island of Eleuthera. Despite the unspectacular weather in London, the Prince and Princess looked much happier than when they left on 17th February, but then, the holiday had ended in better circumstances than it had started.

To begin with their private plans had leaked out to the Press who by the time they left had discovered that they had booked their flight incognito – as Mr and Mrs Hardy – and the Princess' attitude to the 50 or more photographers who waited to see them leave was distinctly cold. A strike of ground staff at Heathrow had also threatened to upset the departure, but airport workers made a last minute decision to suspend it and 200 of them gave the royal couple a rousing cheer into the bargain. Once onto the plane their troubles were not over: several photographers had got to Eleuthera ahead of them and were ready and waiting to take photographs of them sunbathing a couple of days later in the supposed seclusion of Windermere's private beach. There was an enormous row when the pictures appeared in the *Sun* and *Daily Star*, with the other Fleet Street papers joining the Queen, Parliament and the Press Council in deploring the intrusion. The offending papers were quick to publish doubtfully-worded apologies and the Press Council later condemned their actions as a "gross invasion of privacy."

The press intrusion was not the first they had suffered: the previous December photographers caught the Prince and Princess in an embrace at Highgrove, and this and other pictures of the Princess shopping in Tetbury prompted the Queen to complain to newspaper editors at Buckingham Palace.

MARCH 1982

on 20th October at the end of their eight-day visit to New Zealand (opposite page, bottom left). But some of the Queen's engagements at home call not only for evening clothes but also for a degree of splendour and formality in her dress which almost equals the sumptuousness of her appearance on State occasions.

At one such function – a reception at the Savoy Hotel, London on 30th November to mark the 316th anniversary of the founding of the Royal Scottish Corporation – she wore some of her most impressive diamonds, including the famous

Someone, somewhere presumably has a record of the number of evening gowns the Queen has ever worn, but whether this is so or not, it is a good bet that no vision of the Queen comes so readily to mind as one of her fully attired in formal evening dress and glittering with one or other of her fabulous collection of pieces of jewellery.

For the Queen's evening gowns are almost legendary, not only for the number of them she has worn in her thirty-year reign but also for the grand style which, though often predictable, complements the Queen's own

sense of occasion and avoids the cheap, momentarily dramatic effect. With her small figure and her faintly reticent demeanour, she is careful to choose clothes which are colourful without being gaudy, finely made without being extravagant, sparkling without being flashy.

The tendency is to connote the Queen's evening gowns with State occasions – the dinners, banquets and balls which punctuate the State Visits to this country of foreign rulers, or her own official visits abroad – for example the banquet she and Prince Philip gave in Auckland

tiara with the interchangeable pearl drops, and the Sash and Star of the Order of the Thistle (pictures left and right). Her plain, peach-coloured satin dress avoided competition with the heavy jewellery and intricate, watered-silk family orders.
The gala occasion, such as the annual Royal Variety

Performance in November (opposite page, top left) and the Royal Film Première – the Queen attended "Evil Under the Sun" at the Odeon, Leicester Square on 22nd March (opposite page, far left) – also invites the addition of tiara and jewels, though they are less conspicuous on slightly more informal occasions, like the opening of the Barbican Centre on 3rd March (opposite page, bottom left), and her attendance at the film "Absence of Malice" on 21st February (top and left).

MARCH 1982

The Prince and Princess of Wales provided the newly opened Barbican Centre in the City of London with its second royal visit on successive evenings, on 4th March, the day on which the Centre first opened to the public. The concert – or more accurately, the evening of variety entertainment – was staged by the Knights of the Order of St John and appropriately called "Night of Knights." It was held in aid of both the Order and the Prince's Trust, founded under Prince Charles' auspices to assist children and youth groups in disadvantaged areas.

The occasion, in a building whose history had already

broken several records, was the most expensive of its kind in the annals of London public entertainment. Tickets were priced at between £50 and £250 each – causing last minute headaches as over five hundred of them were unsold ten days before the night – but the royal guests made it all more than worthwhile. The Princess, sumptuously dressed in a long cerise evening gown with a deep *fichu* neckline, was lively and animated, chatting with many of the stars of the show, including David Frost, George Burns, Elaine Page and singer Tony Bennett, though she was forced to leave for a short while for a breath of fresh air after waiting under the hot glare of the television lights. But she

returned to a champagne buffet and enjoyed the show in which Mike Yarwood, impersonating Prince Charles (rumour has it that the Prince keeps feeding him tips on how to improve) said that the Princess of Wales had entered a Diana lookalike competition and won third prize. Whether the Prince and Princess had vetted and approved the script beforehand is not known, but they both took the now famous impersonation in good part. It was odds on that Prince Charles would anyway, with his mature and generous sense of humour, and his admission that "if I were not able to see the funny side of life, I would have been committed to

silver and scarlet uniform, and by Royal Fanfare Trumpeters in gold-braided crimson tunics, who heralded her arrival. Accompanied by the Lord Mayor of London, Sir Christopher Leaver, she unveiled a commemorative plaque (on which incidentally some of the colours in the City of London crest were wrong), and in front of an audience of 3,500 people acclaimed the building as "surely having some claim as one of the wonders of the modern world." She toured a couple of art exhibitions – one of paintings, the other of tapestries – and divided the remainder of her time between a concert in the Barbican Hall and

conceived in the heady, enterprising days of the late 1960s when its estimated cost was less than £20 million. By the time of its completion, in the recession-bound Britain of 1981, the total cost had soared to £153 million. But the vision to transform the 20-year-old bombed site into the most comprehensive and lavish conference and arts complex in Western Europe progressed towards materialisation despite years of controversy, delays and accusations that the City Corporation were creating a white elephant. In what even former critics concede as a remarkable achievement, the 11-year project – the largest and

ceiling and hardboard under the seats, gives it the best possible acoustic qualities. The foyer is luxuriant and welcoming, the restaurant alive with vivid and busy decor.
The two royal visits sent this "Xanadu on the Circle Line" as one newspaper editorial put it, well on its way. In the five days of special celebrations – classical and pop concerts, radio entertainments, Ed Stewart's Cockney Morning and a host of informal events in the foyer, the Centre's box office was hopelessly over-subscribed. Queues were twenty deep, switchboards were jammed, the whole building swarmed with people jockeying for access into

an institution long ago." At any rate the proceedings were as pleasantly amicable as the previous evening's business had been formal and full of significance.
That evening, the Queen had formally opened the Barbican Centre amid glittering pageantry. The foyer was lined with pikemen and musketeers in

a Shakespearian-inspired dramatic entertainment, "Swan's Down Gloves," in the Barbican Theatre.
The Lord Mayor said that "the City is adding a new dimension to its life and history" in creating the Centre, and he must certainly have been thinking of the past dozen years when he said it. For the idea was

most expensive into which ratepayers have ever poured funds – now houses the London Symphony Orchestra, the Royal Shakespeare Company and the Guildhall School of Music and Drama. The theatre seats almost 1,200 people; the concert hall over 2,000. The latter has a stage in Baltic pinewood, which, with perspex dishes at the

auditoria or merely content to stand and stare at the immensity and grandeur of it all. The initial rush caused all sorts of administrative problems but no-one was complaining about the success of the enterprise, which as the Queen said, "would be justified by the uses to which it will be put in the future."

MARCH 1982

On 4th March the Queen paid one of comparatively few visits to Newmarket – not to watch racing but to attend the annual Stallion Show staged by the Hunters' Improvement and the National Light Horse Breeding Society. The Queen is Patron of the Society but this was her first official visit to the Show, which encourages the continuation of breeding excellence in this country by the award of the King George V Gold Cup.
The Society was founded almost a hundred years ago, long before the days when Britain's acknowledged and envied supremacy in thoroughbred

she strives for perfection within her own stud.
The event takes place every March at Tattersall's Park Paddocks, a spacious compound just off Newmarket High Street, bounded by rustling poplars and redolent at any time of the year of peaceful countryside with its expansive lawns, white painted railings, rangy stable blocks and tall, wide, grandiose, brick-built sales room which eight or ten times a year echoes to the shout and whinny of Europe's prime auctions of foals, yearlings, mares in foal, horses in training and occasionally stallions. The whiff of horse and straw in this

who introduced to her the usual waiting group of local dignitaries and executives of the host Society. She was then escorted, via the Tattersall's Rooms, to the Royal Box from which she watched, at various intervals throughout the day, the judging of different classes and groups of competitors. These were organised according to geographic districts and the Queen saw the judging of Class 4 (Wiltshire, Gloucestershire and Oxfordshire) and Class 6 (Dorset, Devon and Cornwall) before presenting awards to the respective winners. She also watched a parade of registered

horse breeding went into decline. In the last quarter of a century the alarming increase in the export of representatives of some of the very best bloodlines to the United States and Japan, has put increasing pressure on breeders to maintain the strength of Britain's prestige

during years of comparative hardship. The Queen, who in over thirty years has still not managed to achieve her avowed aim "to breed a horse that wins the Derby" (the one classic race which also eluded her father King George VI) will be in entire sympathy with the aims as

close season for sales was today as welcome to breeders and potential breeders as on any day in the long course of the autumn sales season.
The Queen arrived at the showground by car and was greeted by the Lord Lieutenant of Suffolk, Sir Joshua Rowley,

stallions and, towards the end of the day, a parade of Super Premium Stallions. The Henry Tudor Cup, for the stallion gaining winning marks for "service and foaling returns" – a fairly down-to-earth description of what is expected - was presented by the Queen to Mrs

Margot Peacock of Chester, for her stallion Politico.

As the stud season was in its third week, some of the horses were in a frisky mood and a number of otherwise beautifully turned out animals – groomed to the sleekest shine, tails combed and bandaged, manes bobbed and plaited – played up badly at all the wrong moments. But the day was understandably one of some tension for horses and their owners alike. Not so, however, for the Queen, for whom the four-hour visit was one of great interest to her – very much her sort of event, marred only by the bitterly cold

also discovered that he had jarred his legs during the race and learned that the horse would never run again.

But her interest in the perfection-orientated world of flat racing was already kindled – at about the time, incidentally, that the Queen Mother was persuaded to take an interest in National Hunt racing. She appreciated that success on the flat went hand in hand with the indispensable requirement of efficient breeding, and after her accession to the Throne she maintained a commanding personal interest in the fortunes of the Royal Stud. At that time,

wind which obliged her to keep well wrapped up in her cape for most of the day. And with it went a lunch back at the Tattersall's Rooms, cooked by teenage students from the Isle of Ely Catering College at Wisbech, forty miles away. They served the Queen and seventy other guests a delicious meal of chicken fillets in Madeira sauce with fresh asparagus, followed by Crème Brûlée with oranges. The Queen's undisguised enjoyment at Newmarket has its roots in her early childhood. The Royal Family's great love of horses – some have criticised it as almost an obsession – seems to have inspired all its members to take to the saddle at one time or another. For the Queen, riding has been only a part of her devotion to horses. When she was in her early teens she was taken to the stables of Fred Darling who trained King George VI's horses at Beckhampton in Wiltshire. There she saw and admired horses whose victories in four of

the five Classics races of 1942 gave her a thrill and sense of involvement which has never left her. After the war, the King leased Blue Train from the National Stud and 19-year-old Princess Elizabeth, as she was then, saw him win the Newmarket Stakes. Sadly, she

many horses raced by the Queen, and by her father before her, were leased from the National Stud which until fifteen years ago kept mares as well as stallions, breeding from them and retaining the best stock for next generation matings. (Nowadays, the Stud keeps stallions only, dispensing nominations at the going rate to owners wanting to send their mares for mating.) The leasing arrangement with the royal owners worked to everyone's satisfaction, perhaps never more than when Carrozza, a National Stud filly, won the Oaks for the Queen and contributed strongly to making Her Majesty the winning owner of 1957, with total prize money of over £62,000. This was the second and, to date, last time the Queen has topped the owners' list. Another National Stud product, Hopeful Venture, won the Grand Prix de St Cloud for the Queen in 1968.

Since the leasing scheme came to an end, the Queen has enjoyed proportionately fewer successes on the turf, but many victories repaid the foresight of her ancestors. King Edward VII

daughter Highclere won the 1,000 Guineas as well as the French Oaks. The Queen was at Chantilly to see her win and to lead her to the enclosure amid delirious acclamation from the French racing fraternity who milled round the Queen and caused fears for her safety. Much of the Queen's horse breeding and racing success must be credited to her trainers, the late Cecil Boyd-Rochfort and Lord Porchester, and to her stud managers, Richard Shelley, Michael Oswald and the renowned Captain Charles Moore, who was first engaged by King George VI in 1937 and who taught the Queen much of her basic knowledge of bloodlines. It was he who decided to buy the mare Malapert for only 100 guineas in 1949, mate her with Palestine, to breed Pall Mall, winner of the

renewed royal passion for thoroughbreds and breeding, after Queen Victoria had resurrected the tradition of royal patronage by founding the Hampton Court Stud. From it her son and heir produced the eventual Derby winners Persimmon and Diamond Jubilee – and laid the foundations from which his successor could build. King George V, however, had few winners in his 25-year reign, but in 1934 he bought the mare Feola for 3,000 guineas. It was,

in the event, an act of faith, the consequence of which was that his second son George VI saw a regular procession of winning performances from Feola's offspring, including the almost sanctified Hypericum, who won the 1,000 Guineas in 1946, and Angelola who won the Yorkshire Oaks. She bred Aureola, the Queen's best ever Derby chance, who came second to the legendary Pinza in the 1953 Derby. The long-term influence of Feola was felt as recently as 1974 when her great-grand-

2,000 Guineas for the Queen in 1958. But the Queen's own unflagging interest makes their success possible. She has studied the Form Book assiduously and has made no secret of her passion for the sport of Kings. The short clip from the film "Royal Family" which showed the Queen and Prince Philip travelling by air from one engagement to another – the Duke preparing a formal speech and the Queen reading the latest available copy of *The Sporting Life* – was telling as well as a touch humorous. She has attended auctions at Newmarket and at Doncaster, and not always as a mere spectator. She has herself selected horses in the auction ring and come away with winning mares – like Stroma, whom she bought early in her reign at Doncaster Bloodstock Sales and who bred Canisbay, the winner of the Eclipse Stakes in the late 1960's and a successful stallion at stud since. In addition the Queen has constantly supported her well-chosen breeding management to the point that, since she took over the Wolferton Stud in Norfolk from King George VI, the Stud has produced over three hundred winners in this country alone, bringing home prize money of over half a million pounds. It is a creditable record, and one of which her

great-grandfather King Edward VII would have been justifiably proud.

Having said that, the Queen's best year recently was Silver Jubilee Year, when her filly Dunfermline won the Epsom Oaks and the St Leger at Doncaster – the two prime classics for fillies. Five years have passed without the degree of good fortune in breeding or racing which stamped the early years of her reign with success after success. And the Derby still remains to be won. Perhaps 1983 will help to keep the record respectable – and a smile on the royal features.

MARCH 1982

The Forestry Commission was established just after the First World War with the main aim of ensuring that in any future national emergency the country could depend on essential and immediate supplies of wood. Since then, from the wholesale replanting of hillsides and scrubland in all parts of the United Kingdom has emerged a singular combination of regular supply, landscaping, recreation and amenity, education and research which has made the Commission one of the most widespread, successful and popular nationalised going concerns of the century. Westonbirt Arboretum is a 600-

which to the uninitiated excludes mainly the evergreen types – pines, spruces, firs etc – which are more popularly and more readily associated with the work of the Forestry Commission throughout the British Isles. Some of the Arboretum's trees were planted by the founder Robert Holford a century and a half ago. Others are still being added as each month goes by.

The Commonwealth Forestry Association, which has enjoyed royal patronage throughout its sixty year history, decided that its jubilee should be commemorated by the planting of a new collection of trees in the

an Oregon ash sapling. After the planting ceremonies Prince Charles was taken through the Arboretum by Sir David Montgomery, the Chairman of the Forestry Commission, and Mr D R Johnston, Chairman of the Commonwealth Forestry Association. He toured the Visitor Centre, meeting the staff responsible for the administration and practical running of the Arboretum, and was presented with a splendidly finished carved wooden model of a salmon (pictured below) given to him by nine-year-old Sally Snell, the daughter of a forestry research worker (top picture) as

acre woodland in the heart of Gloucestershire, established privately in the reign of King George IV but for the last quarter of a century managed by the Research and Development Commission of the Forestry Commission. It is also only a stone's throw from Highgrove House, which probably explains

why Prince Charles, who spent the weekend of 6th/7th March there, agreed to visit the Arboretum on the 5th, to celebrate the Diamond Jubilee of the Commonwealth Forestry Association.

The Arboretum contains around 13,000 specimens, principally temperate broadleaved trees,

Arboretum, and Prince Charles was invited to plant on its behalf a red maple, one of several species of maple from Commonwealth countries which will form that collection. Other trees in the collection are, or will include, eucalyptus, oak and Indian horse-chestnut.

Whilst on the site Prince Charles was taken to see two other collections of trees. One was planted to commemorate the Queen's Silver Jubilee in 1977, the other established in 1981 to commemorate his own wedding to Lady Diana Spencer. The collection is not yet complete – only about 15 trees have so far been planted out of a projected total of forty-five or fifty – but the intention is to add as many specimens, out of a total of 65 different species of ash, as are compatible with the local environment. As his contribution the Prince planted

well as a bunch of flowers presented by one of the research workers Mrs Catherine Beard, which he seemed unable to decide what to do with. Before leaving he joined the staff and distinguished guests for tea at the Centre.

The Royal Wedding collection of ash trees should look impressive in their eventual maturity, and must comprise the largest arboreal commemoration of the Royal Wedding. Though they will not match the whole Israeli hillside of forest given to the Queen and Prince Philip to mark their Silver Wedding in 1972, they will put those other famous plantings – those performed at Broadlands in May 1981 and at Hyde Park the following November – well into the shade.

MARCH 1982

"The difference a year makes" has been a constant theme of comments about the Princess of Wales, who has not only risen from relative obscurity to the position of third lady in the land within an incredible short time, but has achieved that unbelievable degree of maturity which gives the impression that she was born to that position. One year, almost to the day, before these pictures were taken, Lady Diana Spencer made her first *coup de théâtre* at Goldsmiths Hall wearing a low-cut black taffeta evening dress which has since become almost legendary. Now, on 8th March 1982 she increased her tally of solo engagements when she paid an evening visit to the Victoria Palace Theatre in London to attend a special charity preview of the play "The Little Foxes."

For a solo engagement it had all the makings of a risky experience involving as it did Britain's most dazzling addition to the Royal Family for years – almost a folk heroine in her own right – and the legendary lady of the screen, known variously as the queen of Hollywood and the superstar of show business, Elizabeth Taylor. On top of that it was lost on no-one that Miss Taylor's leading role in "The Little Foxes" was her British stage début, and that the Princess of Wales was almost as much a novice in her role. So everyone was out to be on their best behaviour.

The Princess arrived attended by her senior lady in waiting, Anne Beckwith-Smith (opposite page, left). Under her brilliant white fur jacket she was stunningly dressed in a long, white and champagne-coloured evening gown with puffed and gathered sleeves, glittering with sprays of sequins. Her much favoured low-cut neckline was set off by an ornate diamond necklace, and she looked happy and very fit and tanned after her recent Bahamian holiday. On her arrival she was presented with a bouquet and a toy fox (opposite page right) by 9-year-old

Caroline O'Neill: a moving moment, since her father, a police constable, was stabbed to death on duty two years ago. The evening's show was in aid of the Metropolitan Police Benevolent Fund and the Army Benevolent Fund.

As guest of honour the Princess was introduced formally to the theatre management and the officials of the two charities, before being escorted to the Royal Box. Here she faltered, unsure as to when precisely to

move into the Box, so that while the State Trumpeters began their fanfare to greet her arrival the spotlight fell on a cluster of empty seats. Eventually, with that apologetic blush which disarms all critics, she made her entry and, amid great applause, took her seat.

The show went without a hitch. Miss Taylor's performance left audience and critics spellbound and the play's producer Zev Bufman said it was "the greatest show she had put on."

"Something special," he called it. The Princess thought it special too: she applauded enthusiastically as the cast took several curtain calls, and roared with laughter when a Welsh Guardsman went onto the stage to present a bouquet to Miss Taylor just as the curtain descended upon him.

Afterwards the Princess met members of the cast and realised her long-held hope that she would one day meet its leading lady. Miss Taylor was in vivid white, and the two of them looked of equal rights. They shook hands; the Princess said how much she had enjoyed the show and thanked her for "such a lovely performance." When, eventually, she had to go, she made her way confidently to the door and was applauded by the cast as she did so. Miss Taylor made as if to follow her, imitating the same striding exit. The Princess looked back: the Queen of Hollywood was caught in the act, and both burst out laughing.

"The Princess was charming, gracious and beautiful," Miss Taylor said afterwards. "I was more than thrilled to meet her." For everyone, it seemed, the evening was "something special."

MARCH 1982

Three generations of the Royal Family have been closely associated with what was originally called the Antique Dealers' Fair since its earliest days at Grosvenor House in the 1930's. Queen Mary, an inveterate gatherer of antiques, visited it as a matter of course – a fact evidenced by the inclusion in the 1982 exhibition of the ornate rosewood tea caddy which she bought there in 1937. The tea caddy now belongs to the Queen Mother, who as present Patron of the fair, loaned it for the purpose.

Today it is called the Burlington

House Fair, having moved to the Royal Academy of Arts in Piccadilly in 1980. On 11th March 1982, Princess Margaret who last opened the Fair in 1971, returned to open the most expansive and expensive of all its forty odd predecessors. Now accommodated in ten galleries, and nearly twice the size of the 1981 Fair, this year's exhibition was a feast of superlatives. Sixty dealers were offering for sale pieces worth more than £50 million. Seventeen advisory committees scrutinised every article to guarantee authenticity.

There was everything from paintings to porcelain, glass and delicate silver to scientific instruments. The customary exhibition of loans, under the title "Connoisseurship & Collecting" displayed articles from the Queen's collection of paintings, the Duke and

Duchess of Kent's silverware, and Princess Alexandra's jewellery, as well as a gallery of pictures by Thomas Rowlandson, the 19th century artist who specialised in painting auction scenes.

Princess Margaret, who takes a close interest in the Fair from year to year, was fascinated by the display, and although her glasses may not become collector items in quite the same way, their appearance was rare enough to invite a certain amount of fascination too.

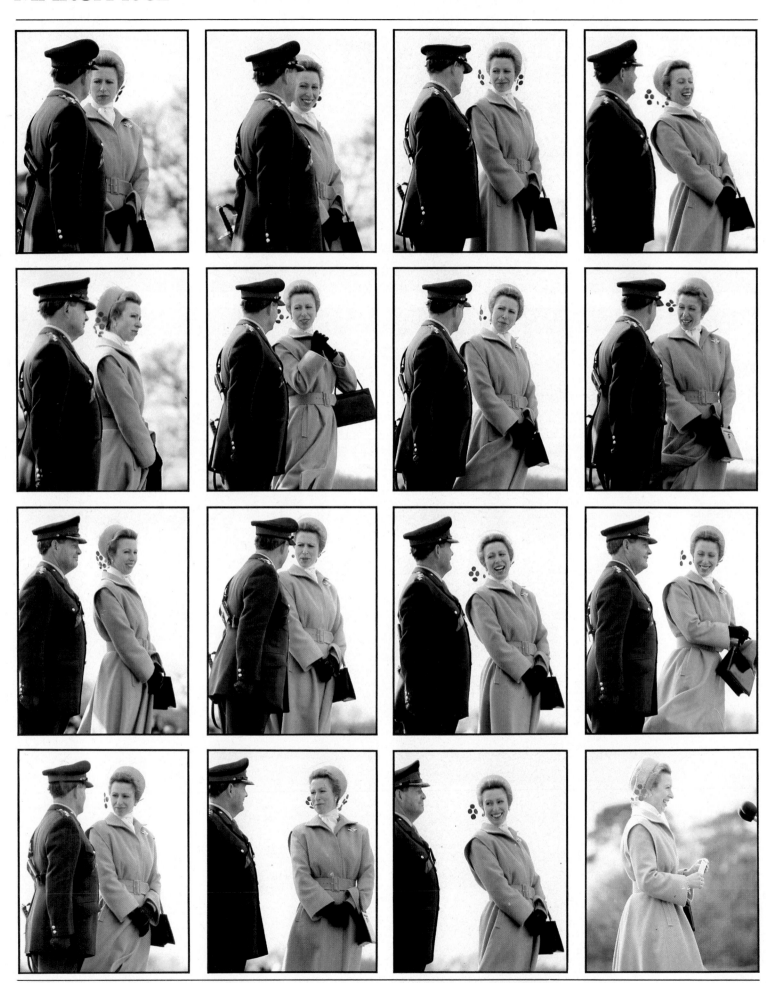

When Princess Anne married Captain Mark Phillips in November 1973 he took her, after their enviable South American honeymoon, to his married quarters, Oak Grove House, at the Royal Military Academy Sandhurst. They didn't stay there long, moving into Gatcombe Park in 1977 just

before Mark left the Army. As Colonel-in-Chief of three regiments it was probably only a matter of time before she was invited back to her husband's old stamping ground and she did indeed accept an invitation to inspect the passing-out parade of Academy graduates on 12th March.

The parade was a comparatively small one, only 89 student officers taking part. They had just graduated from Direct Course No 19, after a twenty-

week training which began in October 1981 and ended with today's confirmed commissions. The ceremonial which surrounded the royal inspection was predictable in character, highly musical and spectacularly enjoyable. A succession of musical marches accompanied the March-on Parade of Amiens and Ypres Companies, before the approach of Princess Anne and her arrival at the reviewing dais to the strains of the National Anthem. During her inspection (far left and centre left) she drew a smile from one bandsman, Sergeant Major Gordon Saunders, whom she recognised as having played for her when she lived at Sandhurst (top left). She returned to the dais for the March Past (bottom pictures) – a lengthy business involving seven changes of music, during which she found time for chirpy conversation with Colonel J E M Hughes, the College Commander of Victory College (opposite page). Princess Anne made a short closing address (opposite page bottom right) remembering her days at Sandhurst with affection, and presented the Commander's Medal to 2nd Lieutenant Andrew Gregory, the best of his course.

One newspaper called it the "laughing-out" parade. It was good to see Princess Anne, whose relationships with the Press are not always cordial, thoroughly enjoying herself for all to see.

Central London came tolerantly to a halt on the morning of 16th March as final preparations were completed for the first State Visit to Britain of His Majesty Sultan Qaboos bin Said Al Said of Oman. Persistent heavy rain in the early morning yielded before his arrival, but overcast skies made it certain that the processions from Victoria Station would be in closed carriages, as happened for the State Visit of the Nigerian President a year previously. Detachments of Household Cavalry (below) and massed

bands (left) paraded from barracks to route positions in capes and greatcoats, only the Kings Troop, Royal Horse Artillery (bottom left) sporting their resplendent gold braided uniforms as they rode towards Hyde Park to give the customary gun salutes.

The Sultan suffered his own experience of the British weather when his VC10 aircraft, preparing to land at Gatwick, was struck on the nose cone by what was described as a severe bolt of lightning, which jolted the plane's passengers but otherwise did no harm. "I've heard of 21-gun salutes," said the pilot, Denis Lowry, "but that was ridiculous." None the worse for his shock, the Sultan was greeted at Gatwick by the Duke of Gloucester and calmly emerged from the aircraft to join the Royal Train for Victoria. For many State Visitors to Britain, this habitual welcoming protocol is strange and novel,

but the Sultan would have understood it better than most. He has been a regular visitor – on semi-official as well as on several private occasions – to the country towards which he feels great affection. It was to Britain that he was sent at the age of 18 in 1958 to study privately in Suffolk before going to Sandhurst in 1960 and joining the 1st Battalion, the Cameronians, with BAOR in West Germany in 1962. It was with the aid of British officers that he overthrew his severely feudal father in 1970, after spending years in prison in Dhofar province, and the British came to his assistance three years later to put down an insurrection there, inspired by his Marxist neighbours in South Yemen (formerly British Aden). Sultan Qaboos, who owns a country house in Berkshire, loves Britain and has immense admiration and respect for the Royal Family.

His welcoming by the Queen and Prince Philip at Victoria Station (this page) was as much a personal greeting as a significant gesture in the history of the relations between Britain and Oman. As a token of his personal regard for the Queen, the Sultan had brought with him

Engineering of Clydebank disclosed a £50 million order for gas turbines for Oman's new power station. For Prince Philip (left) the welcoming ceremonies at Victoria Station carried an even more personal element, since less than a month previously he had been the Sultan's guest during his short trip to Oman as President of the World Wildlife Fund.

Other members of the Royal

an 18ct gold insignia, studded with diamonds and rubies, which the makers, Spink and Sons of London, ventured to think was probably the richest of its kind anywhere in the world. As a token of the more practical faith which the Sultan has in British technology, his visit coincided with the

announcement that he had concluded a £215 million contract with Cementation International to build a University in Oman, with the possible benefit of ancillary equipment and services worth £140 million to be provided by British firms, and before the end of the visit, John Brown

Family were also there to greet the Sultan – amongst them Princess Anne and Captain Mark Phillips (overleaf with the Duchess of Gloucester) and the Duke and Duchess of Kent (bottom right). There was a slight hitch in the welcoming ceremonies when it was discovered that Baroness Phillips, the Lord Lieutenant of London – who was supposed to introduce the Sultan to the Prime Minister – had not arrived. Apparently her newly-employed chauffeur failed to collect her from home. But protocol notwithstanding, the

MARCH 1982

Prime Minister, along with her Cabinet colleagues Foreign Secretary Lord Carrington and Home Secretary Mr William Whitelaw (below right), were duly introduced. They met again the following day at Downing Street, where Mrs Thatcher entertained the Sultan to lunch, and had "extremely friendly and cordial talks."

The journey from Victoria Station, preceded by the Sultan's inspection of the Guard of Honour, was not without incident. Just as the Queen and her guest, with Prince Philip, were leaving in the Irish State Coach, a brown Renault 16 was spotted parked in the Mall between Clarence House and Buckingham Palace. Suspecting the worst, police quickly flashed a message to the procession organisers to detour through Birdcage Walk while the car was detonated by a small controlled

The Sultan's afternoon programme followed the usual pattern – an address of welcome by the Lord Mayor of Westminster at St. James's Palace, a courtesy visit to the Queen Mother at Clarence House, and a visit to Westminster Abbey to lay a wreath on the grave of the Unknown Warrior. That evening the Queen gave a State Banquet at Buckingham Palace which the whole of the Royal Family, save Prince Andrew, Prince Edward, Princess Alice and Princess Alexandra and her husband, attended. In her speech the Queen admitted that Britain had

explosion – which revealed that it was harmless. Its owner, Michael Waterfield of Canterbury, had parked it there without realising what concern it would cause, and he later commemorated the fact by insisting that the dent in his boot, caused by the detonation, should not be knocked out. Meanwhile, however, thousands of people, many Omanis included, who had waited in the Mall for a glimpse of the royal visitor, were disappointed.

been criticised for losing interest in the Arabian peninsula but promised that "we shall keep faith with Oman."

After visiting the Prime Minister the following day, Sultan Qaboos was guest of honour at the Lord Mayor's luncheon at the Guildhall, at which the Duke of Kent was present. It was here that the Sultan made his most overtly political speech of the entire visit, condemning "Soviet imperialist interference in the Arab World" which "exploits the situation for its own ends." He urged a peaceful solution to the Palestinian problem on the basis of an honourable settlement of the plight of the Palestinians "in the interests of justice and common humanity" and was "convinced that our friends in the West have an important responsibility...in solving the problems that confront the Middle East today."

Considering how vulnerable Oman is in an area of seething international politics and vital commercial importance to the world economy, his words were both implacable against potential enemies and logically attractive towards friends. For in addition to the mainland of Oman, the Sultan rules a small triangle of land just to the north

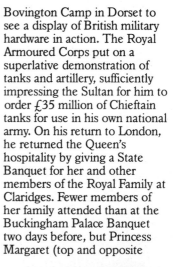

east of the United Arab Emirates, which controls the Straits of Hormuz through which every oil tanker must pass from the Persian Gulf. He confidently promised his Guildhall hosts that all the Western World's oil which sails through the Straits to keep their economies alive, would continue to do so, and paid tribute to the contribution that Britain had made towards bringing Oman out of the backward state in which he had inherited it in

1970. In those days there was hardly a metalled road in the whole country. Now it fairly bristles with beautifully tarmac'd desert roads, airports, schools, clinics, factories, electricity systems and television. And in the forces, the process of Omanisation – the gradual handover of knowhow and leadership from the invited British forces to the Omanis – has taken its first tentative steps. The last full day of the Sultan's visit was taken up by a visit to

Bovington Camp in Dorset to see a display of British military hardware in action. The Royal Armoured Corps put on a superlative demonstration of tanks and artillery, sufficiently impressing the Sultan for him to order £35 million of Chieftain tanks for use in his own national army. On his return to London, he returned the Queen's hospitality by giving a State Banquet for her and other members of the Royal Family at Claridges. Fewer members of her family attended than at the Buckingham Palace Banquet two days before, but Princess Margaret (top and opposite

page left) and the Duchess of Gloucester (right) enhanced the occasion with their richly coloured evening gowns and sparkling jewellery. As did the Queen, who was delighted to be welcomed personally by the Sultan in this colourful finale to a most satisfactory visit.

The British Royal Family's amicable personal relations with Oman's Sultan has parallels with other tribal or hereditary rulers. Perhaps the best example is the Nepalese monarchy whose

present head King Birendra is a close personal friend of Prince Charles. The Prince, with his great-uncle Lord Mountbatten attended the King's coronation at Katmandu in 1975, and visited the King during his solo tour in December 1980. The Duke and Duchess of Gloucester spent a fortnight or so in Nepal in February 1982. Neighbouring Thailand's King Bhumibhol and Queen Sirikit

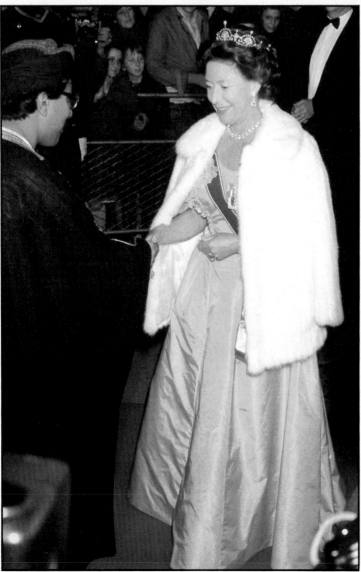

are also great friends of the Queen, who hosted them during their State Visit to Britain in 1960 and paid her own State Visit to Bangkok in 1972. Members of the Thai Royal Family were guests of the Queen during Royal Ascot week in 1980.

Of the small tribal African monarchs, King Sobhuza II of

Swaziland enjoys the strongest personal ties with the British Royal Family. Princess Alexandra attended Swaziland's independence celebrations in 1969 and in September 1981 Princess Margaret conferred the Order of St Michael and St George – Britain's highest foreign award – on the 82-year-old King during his diamond jubilee celebrations.

MARCH 1982

Royal engagements at home do not stop when a foreign Head of State visits Britain and on 17th March, the second day of the Sultan of Oman's four-day stay, Prince Philip added another three official functions to his impressive list. One of his duties was to accompany the Queen to the Authors of the Year party at New Zealand House; another was, as Colonel-in-Chief of the Queen's Royal Irish Hussars, to attend the St Patrick's Day Parade at Tidworth. And that evening he attended a dinner given at the Inn on the Park in London, in aid of the St John Ambulance Brigade and of the

Duke of Edinburgh's Award Scheme.

As these pictures show, Prince Philip thoroughly enjoyed himself at this latter function when the presentation of cheques (opposite page, bottom) seemed almost incidental to the after dinner speeches, which were full of witty repartee. BBC newsreader Jan Leeming (opposite page) seemed to be in almost as good form as the Prince himself, whose own speech included hilarious references to the unspeakable character "Dirty

George," the current toast of American cable Television.
The Duke of Edinburgh's Award Scheme, now twenty-six years old, has the distinction of being one of those few entirely voluntary enterprises to have enjoyed nothing but success since its inception – and that to such an extent that the Post Office issued a set of commemorative stamps to celebrate its Silver Jubilee in 1981. Its growth is particularly remarkable in the light of its unpromising start, when for three years the number of

and the relative freedom of adulthood. But the Scheme embraces voluntary assistance and co-operation of adults outside that age range, for unpaid administrative and advisory support is essential to its continuing success.
But the Scheme differs from many others in that it is not confined to outdoor activity. Reflecting the Duke's own recent words that "the great outdoors means different things

annual entrants failed to rise above the initial 8,000 mark. Then everything took off. By 1960 the yearly intake reached 20,000; by 1963 there were 65,000; by 1972, 90,000. Now, after a quarter of a century of almost unstoppable increase, over a hundred thousand young people join the scheme every year, and more than 1½ million have taken part since the scheme's inauguration.
Like many of the schemes adopted or sponsored by Prince Philip – the Outward Bound Trust, the Federation of Boys'

Clubs, the Playing Fields Association and the Council for Physical Recreation – the Award Scheme encourages adventure and initiative, recreation and a balanced development among the young. "Young" encompasses those aged between 14 and 25, thus representing the link between the disciplines of school years

to different people" the Scheme is wide enough to incorporate indoor projects, particularly those connected with community service and constructive pastimes.
The Duke personally presents Gold Standard Awards to winners at regular receptions at Buckingham Palace, at the rate of some two to three thousand a year, and if time allows during the course of his tours abroad he will attend similar receptions for Commonwealth award winners who lack the means or opportunity to come to London.

MARCH 1982

The Duchess of Kent's abiding interest in music – she is an accomplished pianist and a member of the Bach Choir – found an outlet on 17th March when she attended a gala concert given by the Royal College of Music Orchestra in aid of the Hampstead Old People's Housing Trust at Merchant Taylor's Hall.

A fortnight later, on 2nd April, the Royal County of Berkshire entertained a royal visitor when the Queen undertook a two-hour tour of the Berkshire County Council headquarters at Shire Hall, Shinfield Park, near

Reading.

It was the first visit by the Queen to Reading, which is only twenty miles from Windsor, for four years, and the first time a reigning sovereign had seen the workings of Berkshire's administration.

Shire Hall, a £27 million building begun over five years before, concentrates the activities of what was originally some sixteen scattered buildings throughout Reading into one well-equipped and efficiently-run headquarters. Its short history has been a controversial one, with attempts to sell off what had at an early stage been realised as an intolerably expensive project, to cope with the reductions in public expenditure which became necessary as the latest recession began to bite. But that was now a thing of the past.

Shire Hall lies only half a mile from the M4 and the route from the intersection to the headquarters was lined by almost five thousand children from over forty schools in the county, with an additional welcome from members of

Berkshire "could justifiably be proud." He mentioned the obvious links between Berkshire and the House of Windsor, which were illustrated on a tapestry behind the Queen. This had been produced by a local school, Bayliss Court, and showed the Shire Hall and Windsor Castle.

The Queen declared the building open. It was a formal ceremony since it had been in use for several months already, as the remainder of the royal visit was to show. There were exhibitions by most of the departments, including the Fire

Guide, Scout and Sea Cadet groups, a disabled persons' club and the Reading Association for the Blind.

In his speech of welcome the County Council Chairman, Mr Lewis Moss, referred to the building as one of which

Brigade, the Planning Department and the Thames Valley Police, and both the Queen and Prince Philip saw staff at work at their desks. The librarians produced a display and the Queen was presented with a facsimile of a Windsor Forest

Plea Roll, seven hundred years old. It recorded that a lady guest of King Edward I at Windsor poached twenty-seven head of deer from the neighbouring forest, and that her husband was summoned to answer for her when she failed to turn up at

Court.

The Queen was also given a copy of "The History of the First Berkshire County Council" and in return she and Prince Philip signed photographs of themselves as well as the Visitors Book.

MARCH 1982

Between the two great personal tragedies of her life – the death of her mother the Duchess of Kent in March 1861, and the death of her husband the Prince Consort the following December – Queen Victoria visited the Army Staff College at Camberley and commemorated the event by planting a tree in its front lawn. On 19th March 1982 her great-great-granddaughter Elizabeth II paid her second visit to the College – her first for twenty-four years – and performed a similar symbolic ceremony by planting a young beech tree in the same lawn

their own way. Apart from the tree planting ceremony – she will have appreciated the link with Queen Victoria's visit – the Queen was introduced to Mr Terence Cuneo who in the 1960s was a regular painter of the Queen, particularly in uniform and on horses. As it happened, he was commissioned to paint a picture of her previous visit to Camberley in 1958 – a painting which the Queen inspected – and was engaged again to portray the 1982 visit. Presumably to hedge their bets, the College officers had also arranged for the Queen and the

(opposite page, bottom). The two companion trees symbolise not only the continuity of monarchy but also the loyalty which has existed in the last two centuries between the Army and the Sovereign, which forms one of the bases of our firmly-established democratic system. As Head of the Armed Forces, the Queen's presence from time to time at one or other Army establishment is, if not *de rigueur,* a highly desirable and logical feature of her official programme. This particular visit, which could easily have been a rather drab affair, was full of little incidents carefully arranged to attract the Queen's interest and attention. The heavier items in the royal schedule involved formal introductions of Liaison Officers from the two other armed forces and the armies of France and Western Germany, and the discussions on law and order, parts of which were attended by the Queen for over half an hour.

The lighter moments were probably more memorable in

Duke of Edinburgh, who accompanied her to Camberley, to pose for an official photograph with the College staff.

After lunch, at which over a hundred people sat down with the Queen and the Duke of Edinburgh in the Staff College Dining Room, and raised their glasses to a toast proposed by the Commander, Major General John Akehurst, the royal visitors were taken to the College's reference library to meet civilian and military administrative staff. The Queen was shown a copy of "The Story of the Staff College, 1858-1958" which had been signed, in the College's centenary year, by one of its royal graduates, Prince Henry, the late Duke of Gloucester who, as the Queen's last

surviving uncle, died in June 1974. Subsequently the Queen and Prince Philip visited Alanbrook Hall Lecture Theatre to see an overseas students' exhibition representing activities and contributions from representatives of some thirty-two different countries. They met some of the overseas students and their wives and the Queen received a bouquet of flowers from Vivian Mumbi, the daughter of one of them (top left).

After a brief but chatty walkabout in the College grounds to meet staff, students and their families (above) the four-hour visit to one of the many branches of a loyal, efficient and reliable Army by its Colonel-in-Chief, was over. At the end of the visit, the Queen and Prince Philip were met by the Mayor of Surrey Heath, Councillor Mrs Joy Reid, and left by the College's main gates for a drive through Camberley. Perhaps there was time to remember the days shortly after their marriage in 1947 when they lived just down the road at Windlesham before moving into Clarence House.

MARCH 1982

The film "Evil Under the Sun" based on the Agatha Christie thriller, was given its first royal boost on 22nd March when the Queen and the Duke of Edinburgh attended a performance of it at the Odeon Cinema, Leicester Square, helping to raise almost £100,000 for the Cinema and Television Benevolent Fund. Three days later the Duchess of Gloucester travelled to Southampton to attend another showing for the Royal Charity Film Evening Gala, which was arranged to benefit the more local charity of the Mountbatten Memorial Trust Romsey Sea Venture.

incidentally could not have inherited her father's title but for a Special Reminder written into the granting of his Earldom, so that the Mountbatten name could be perpetuated through either sex. With them was their eldest son Lord Romsey, who has taken over Mountbatten's home, Broadlands, on the outskirts of Romsey and whose close friendship with Prince Charles ensures the continuation of the long association between his family and the Royal Family. He was accompanied by Lady Romsey, the former Penelope Eastwood (seen far right and bottom pictures with the

The Mountbatten representation that evening was as strong as the various connections between the film and the family. The film's producer is Lord Brabourne – John Brabourne to the film world – the husband of Lord Mountbatten's elder daughter, Countess Mountbatten. Was it really he who allowed the film to be marketed under the caption "Holidays Can Be Murder" – ironic in view of the circumstances in which his father-in-law, son and mother-in-law were killed and he and his wife so badly injured on that tragic August Bank Holiday in 1979? He was there, anyway, at the side of his wife – who

Duchess of Gloucester) who announced three months later that she was expecting her second baby. Foremost amongst the stars introduced to the Duchess was Peter Ustinov – presiding almost avuncularly over the activities of the rest of the cast (centre pictures and opposite page right).

The Mountbatten Memorial Trust was established within only a few weeks of the Earl's death and is administered by members of his family under the chairmanship of his great-nephew the Prince of Wales. Its function is to support those charitable and non-profit-

overlook Horse Guards Parade – any surplus will be handed over to the Trust.

A further memorial to Lord Mountbatten achieved fame at the wedding of the Prince and Princess of Wales, in the form of the golden roses bearing his name which featured conspicuously in the Princess' wedding bouquet. In May 1982, a basket of them was presented to Countess Mountbatten at the Chelsea Flower Show in a short ceremony punctuated by a fanfare from a Marine trumpeter. The profits from the sale of the strain are to be partly paid out to the Soldiers' Sailors' and Airmen's Association, of which Lord Mountbatten was President at the time of his death.

making organisations – like the United World Colleges – to which Lord Mountbatten had given his support or blessing during his life. Three years after his death, the Trust is flourishing and still receives funds from all quarters: only three weeks after the Film Evening Gala at Southampton, Countess Mountbatten received from the Indo-British Cultural Exchange a cheque for £15,000 raised as the result of a performance of the Nritya Natika Ramayana troupe which Prince Charles himself attended. The previous January it was decided that of the £85,000 received from some forty countries to pay for a statue to Lord Mountbatten's memory – the proposed site will

The Special Remainder enjoyed by the Earldom of Mountbatten is a comparative rarity in the British honours system. Its purpose is to ensure that the title does not become extinct when the male line dies out – which is what happens in the case of most peerages. But for the Remainder, Mountbatten's Earldom would have died with him, as he had no sons and no younger brothers through whom the title could devolve. As it is his elder daughter Lady Brabourne became the 2nd Countess Mountbatten and her son Lord Romsey will in due course inherit as the 3rd Earl.

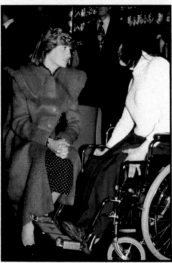

Had it not been for her pregnancy, the Princess of Wales would have been an extremely busy woman in this her first year of marriage to the heir to the Throne. But the fact that she was expecting her first child did not oblige her to cancel all public engagements, as custom had dictated in the past. She merely cut down the schedule which might have been expected of her so as to balance her obvious popularity and the wish of her future subjects to see her, with the need to avoid engagements which were too frequent or strenuous.

The photographs on these pages illustrate a number of different duties she undertook in February and March. One of her earliest engagements of the year was the dinner given by the British Film Institute at 11 Downing Street on 2nd February, for which she wore this superb velvet evening dress with its *fichu* neckline (above). At the end of the month she and Prince Charles joined the Queen Mother (opposite page top left) for a service of thanksgiving for the centenary of the Royal College of Music at Westminster Abbey. This centenary was celebrated again on 14th March with a concert at the Royal Albert Hall (opposite page, bottom pictures).

On 22nd March, visits were arranged at the last minute to Newcastle-upon-Tyne and Huddersfield, where grants were being awarded by the Prince's Trust to assist individuals and social groups of young people in disadvantaged areas. The

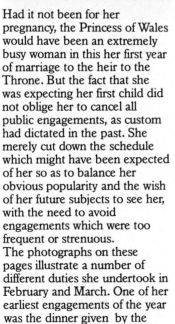

Princess, natural as ever, stopped to discuss problems with some of the recipients over a cup of tea (opposite page, pictures top left) at Huddersfield. And eight days later she divulged what she thought to be her baby's expected date of birth, July 1st, while opening a hospital in Leeds (top right and opposite page, bottom). Everyone instantly latched onto the date as if it were Gospel, despite official reservations from the Palace which ultimately proved well founded.

APRIL 1982

A hundred and fifty years ago Britain negotiated the Peace of Nanking with Imperial China after a comparatively brief skirmish over the opium trade. The terms were favourable to Britain: reparations of £5¾ million, the opening of five Chinese ports to British trade, and the cession of Hong Kong. Immediately, the Royal Navy recruited Hong Kong sailors into her ships and once in Britain many of them eventually settled in the great bustling, north-western port of Liverpool. The descendants of some of those Chinese recruits were presented on 2nd April 1982 to the Prince and Princess of Wales, who arrived in their maroon Rolls-Royce to perform the official opening of the Pagoda of the Hundred Harmonies on the outskirts of the City's Chinese quarter. It isn't really a pagoda at all, but its design imitates the style as closely as the purpose of the building allows. And the purpose is, quite simply, a community centre, specifically for the oldest Chinese community of its kind in Western Europe, and the second largest, next to London's Soho, in Britain. The Merseyside Chinese thus became the first in Europe to have their very own community building. So the day was one of special pride for them.

There is no getting away from the fact that Merseyside's social history this century has been a tough one. Its communities have been stricken with some of the worst effects of unemployment and poverty when times have been bad, and popular impatience with Central Government has boiled over into violence and disorder: the "Scuffers" strike of 1920, the Depression of the 1920's and 1930's, a whole series of debilitating dock strikes, and more recently the street riots in Toxteth, born, it was thought, out of racial tension and bitterness. But today the mood had changed and the thousands present were out to have a good

before," pulled her towards him and planted a decisive kiss on her cheek, momentarily giving her quite a shock. For her part the Princess made three-year-old Colin Griffiths' day when he slipped between the legs of Special Branch police officers and ran towards her to present his 70p worth of yellow tulips. He turned back towards his mother, then changed his mind and made for the Princess, said "I love you" and smothered her with kisses. As she bent down to hug him, the crowd cheered them both on, thrilled by the spontaneity of it all. "I'm not

day.
Everyone seemed to enter into the spirit of elation, including the Prince and Princess, who were at their most delightfully informal. Prince Charles watched as his wife received a long line of VIPs in the welcoming ceremony, and decided to join the back of the queue. When his turn came he said, "I believe we've met

really surprised at what he did," said his mother afterwards. "He really adores her. She's his favourite person and he loves to watch her on television."
The opening ceremony was typically spectacular. The Prince and Princess each painted-in the eyes of the hundredweight-and-a-half ceramic dragon at the entrance to the building in the

manner of the New Year festivities, when the dragon comes to life. The pagoda's dragon in fact had electric light bulbs for eyes, giving the building a glowing identity at night.

The royal couple toured the centre and saw the Chinese inscription on the outer wall reading: "This community will strive for prosperity, harmony and the aspiration for future multi-racial integration and understanding with all peoples." Remembering Toxteth, they were noble sentiments.

The centre itself realised an aspiration – that of Mr Brian Tai-Sheng Wang, who at only 32 is a full-time Community Liaison Officer and who in the seven years since he arrived from Taiwan has devoted his time to creating the circumstances in which young Chinese might obtain educational and career opportunities. His efforts have placed him in high regard: he did much to secure the £¼ million needed for the centre – £228,000 from the Inner City Partnership, the remainder from local fund-raising events. The Prince and Princess were entertained to an eight-course lunch prepared by cooks from two of Liverpool's Chinese restaurants. It lived up to the reputation of all Chinese meals: there were spare ribs, crispy stuffed phoenix-tail prawns with spring onions, fried duckling with jasmin, sweet and sour fish, chicken in yellow bean sauce and platters of fruits offered by what were mysteriously referred to as "celestial ladies." Over lunch, and during the folk dancing display that accompanied it, the Princess spoke to Mr Wang's 30-year-old wife Nora. As luck would have it she too was expecting a baby – a month earlier than the Princess – so there was plenty to talk about. But Mrs Wang remained inscrutable afterwards: "We talked quite a lot about the sort of thing that ladies like us do talk about." So evidently did Prince Charles. He told Mrs Christine Cheetham and Mrs Jill Walker, both also pregnant: "It must be something in the water." Surely he must know better than that!

APRIL 1982

In the face of the doubtful treatment it meted out to them during the early part of their holiday in the Bahamas, the Prince and Princess of Wales might justifiably feel that they have no cause to bestow any patronage, direct or indirect, upon *The Sun* newspaper. But there's nothing Prince Charles loves better than watching a first class steeplechase and he did happen (if that's the right word) to be in Liverpool on official business the day before the Grand National was due to be run at Aintree. As the Grand National, together with all the other five races on the day's race card, is sponsored by *The Sun,* the Prince was in a dilemma. He chose not to cut off his nose to

appropriate as both the Prince and Princess of Wales have Stuart blood in them (though on different sides of the blanket). But Royal Stuart had been unplaced in all his National Hunt races during the season and the housewives' gift of an estimated £30 million therefore went on the next best alternative Royal Mail – twice winner and once placed in his four races. Good Prospect was also among the thirty-nine runners and the sight of him being walked around the parade ring must have brought to Prince Charles memories of what was and dreams of what ought to have been. For it was with Good Prospect that, just over a year before, his steeplechasing career

came to a halt.

The enthusiasm with which Prince Charles took up racing under National Hunt rules matched the zeal of many past and present members of the Royal Family for the sport of horseracing in its various guises, and his first attempt as a qualified rider revealed considerable promise. In March 1980, riding Long Wharf, he ran in second out of a field of thirteen in the Madhatters Private Sweepstake at Plumpton. There was a sort of prophetic quality about the purpose of the race – the tote proceeds were destined for the Injured Jockeys Benevolent Fund! His next attempt, on a horse called Sea Swell the

spite his face and after lunch on 3rd April he and his wife turned up to watch an absorbing day's racing, along with a crowd of about 80,000 that had been swelled by well publicised knowledge of the royal visit. If the customary belief is true that the presence of a member of the Royal Family at a racecourse sends housewives running to the bookmakers to put money on any horse whose name carried the remotest association with royalty, a few million extra pounds must have changed hands that day. There was Gambling Prince in the 2.00, a choice in the 4.05 of Golden Heritage or Royal Dipper (pretty apt in view of Prince Charles' own steeplechasing career), Charlie Muddle – which seems a bit unkind – in the 4.35, and Cornishman in the 5.05. In the Grand National itself Royal Stuart seemed the most

following September, was a comparative disappointment – the experts said he rode well, but he finished last out of four – and a fair way behind the field at that. From that point, nothing went right for him. He trained for some months on the Queen Mother's gelding Allibar, but the horse collapsed one morning in

February 1981 while being brought back to stables after a morning gallop, and died almost immediately, with the Prince and his fiancée by his side.

The Prince of Wales refused to give up his ambition and selected Good Prospect to be trained at the Lambourn stables of Nick Gaselee, whose daughter Sarah Jane was to be a bridesmaid at his wedding. Prince Charles rode Good Prospect twice within one disastrous week in March. At Sandown he was thrown from his horse and, riding at walking pace, came back to the unsaddling enclosure apologetically and with a bloody nose. Five days later, at the Cheltenham Festival, he fell

once again from Good Prospect and sat helplessly in the middle of the course, thrashing the ground with his crop in a fury of temper and frustration.

He was the first to admit that his fall was his own fault, but was not alone in his self-criticism. A Cheltenham steward said that Prince Charles was nowhere

near good enough for any but elementary National Hunt races and commended him to point-to-point, in which his great-uncle, the late Duke of Windsor, had excelled before being prevailed upon by anxious parents to call a halt for safety's sake. Prince Charles seemed to need no persuading – with his

wedding only four months away and discouraged as much by his fiancée, whose own love of riding turned sour when she was thrown from a horse while still a schoolgirl, as by anyone else, he gave up the quest and settled for the relative gentility of polo! Prince Charles' attendances at race meetings have been comparatively rare in recent months and many people imagine, not without at least the superficial justification of appearances, that this has been in some measure due to his wife's antipathy for the sport. That impression was reinforced just a fortnight before Aintree when the couple went to Cheltenham to watch the race for the Gold Cup. The Princess

appeared uninterested in much of the afternoon's activity and even seemed to cold-shoulder her husband when he tried to cheer her up.

But whatever the impression she gave at Cheltenham, there was no doubting her enjoyment of Aintree. She and her husband were joined by Mrs Gaselee (opposite page, in white hat), the wife of Prince Charles' former trainer, as they watched the earlier races from the balcony above Lord Derby's box – the royal couple had stopped overnight with Lord Derby at his country home at Knowsley – and, as at Cheltenham, Prince Charles was busy with his binoculars (opposite page, bottom left) while his wife was clearly glad of some female company to turn to from time to

time.

With half the spectators dithering between watching the racing and keeping an eye on the royal party, the Prince and Princess decided to move off for the Grand National itself. They hopped into a Range Rover and made for the Canal Turn, where they would be able to see the field jumping the second highest fence of the entire course of thirty obstacles. The Canal Turn has the added advantages of being furthest away from the central enclosures, and thus well clear of curious crowds, and of being one of the fences which the horses would jump twice in the course of the race.

Once established at the Canal Turn, the Prince and Princess

found that they lacked sufficient height to see the race properly, and the few spectators in the area were treated to the unusual sight of the royal couple clambering onto the bonnet of their Range Rover to get a better view. At one point no fewer than four people were perched in this rather precarious position, perhaps the least dignified way in which royalty has voluntarily appeared in public. But it was strictly private, essentially enjoyable, and very informal, with the Princess at one stage casually leaning on Prince Charles' shoulder while sitting on the bonnet of a Land Rover (overleaf), or closely confering over the Race Card – which is not so much a card these days as a 36-page booklet. When it was all over, Prince

APRIL 1982

Charles jumped off the Range Rover, while the Princess sat down and slid off in a less vigorous but equally effective manner.

A lot of horses finished the race riderless, though fortunately their fallen jockeys were not injured in the attempt to achieve steeplechasing's richest and

48, the oldest man ever to have won a Grand National. With that satisfactory record safely under his belt, he declared that he was going to hang up his boots.

He won by 15 lengths on Grittar, a nine-year-old gelding carrying fifth highest weight, and with a past form – three wins and two places in six outings – to match.

most envied prize. The usual mess was made of a lot carefully built fences, and the course was littered with the débris of brushwood and foliage. But it was a good race, memorable not only for its handsomest ever prize money – this year a total of £63,000 was paid out to the owners of the first four horses – £51,000 of it contributed by *The Sun* – but also for some record-breaking personal achievements. Geraldine Rees carried on where pioneer Charlotte Brew left off four years before, and on her 10-year-old horse Cheers became the first woman jockey to complete the entire course since women were admitted as qualifiers under National Hunt rules. And the winner, Dick Saunders, became at the age of

That was a good result for Prince Charles in a way, since he had been tipping Grittar hotly while talking to Liverpudlians during his visit to the city the previous day. And at 7-1, anybody who took the Prince's

advice had a lot to thank him for. Prince Charles, reflecting than a previous Prince of Wales, his great-great-grandfather King Edward VII, owned the Grand National winner Ambush II in 1900, and that his grandmother's chances of duplicating that success slipped tragically away from her as Devon Loch collapsed in the last stages of the 1956 National, may have rued the day he gave up the turf on his own account. But, as the Queen Mother once said: "That's racing." The owners of Aintree racecourse may not have taken

were quarrels about the amount of money which television companies should pay for the right to televise live, and about the level of course-side advertising permitted to be shown during television coverage by the BBC. In the mid 1970's there was a series of rapid-fire deals in which ownership of the course changed

hands several times for millions of pounds, and the future of the Grand National hung in perpetual balance. Eventually the growing phenomenon of commercial sponsorship overtook Aintree and for a time the financial danger was over. The *Daily Star* newspaper lost no time supporting the latest campaign for the Grand

National's survival and enlisted the help of Captain Mark Phillips for the purpose – on the strength of which it claimed that "the Royal Family are backing the *Daily Star* campaign to save the Grand National." Captain Phillips referred to the day in 1979 when, only five hours before the Grand National was due to be run, he "was lucky enough to be asked to jump the Grand National course on Columbus. I was therefore able to experience the unique contours of the ground . . . and the exhilaration of jumping those magnificent fences." He added that they were not the toughest fences he had jumped – most were "fair and straight-forward" and he had been more cunningly challenged by certain fences in cross-country events. But the main thrust of his plea was unmistakeable. "The Grand National at any other site could never be the same due to that ground, and its loss would be tragic not only for the United Kingdom, but for the world of equestrianism." The struggle goes on.

quite such a philosophical view of things that day. They celebrated the Grand National by launching a £7 million appeal to save the course from closing down permanently.
The appeal opened another unfortunate chapter in the life of one of those famous, hallowed repositories of the nation's revered traditions in its attempt to come to grips with the realities of economic life. Aintree, long owned by the controversial Topham family, led by its daunting champion Mrs Mirabel Topham, first showed serious financial cracks in the late 1960's. There were threats to close down the course altogether, and with it the inimitable ambience of the annual Grand National. There

APRIL 1982

The first of three consecutive daily royal visits to Wales took place on 6th April, when Prince Charles carried out a couple of engagements in Glamorganshire. These pictures show him in his usual affable and easygoing mood, meeting local residents and not a few admirers, during a visit to Tondu to open the new Glamorgan Nature Reserve. During his walkabout he received the usual quantities of flowers – appropriately enough he had chosen daffodil time for a Welsh trip – as well as mementoes, like the red dragon (opposite page, lower left) offered to him by one youngster, and a few tips on the subject of babies (opposite page centre left), a topic fast becoming an inevitable element of conversation between the Prince and Princess and the large numbers of people they meet. Earlier Prince Charles had visited the Royal Mint at Llantrisant, in mid-Glamorgan – one of a number of royal visits

time of his Investiture, that he would maintain a deep interest in Wales' future, has fallen by the wayside.

Even the briefest of surveys of the Prince's connections with the Welsh over the last thirteen years shows this impression to be entirely false. An analysis of his visits to the Principality since 1969 reveals that he spends an average of a day there every six weeks – a figure boosted by the two great marathons – the four-

the establishment has received since its removal from London a decade or so ago. Here he saw a large variety of the coins produced for use in this country as well as abroad, together with some proof specimens of the crown piece minted to commemorate his wedding, and

bearing his wife's portrait on it as well as his own.

With one recent and notable exception, Prince Charles' many visits to his Principality are not much publicised these days. The impression may consequently have been given that his intention, much vaunted at the

day tour immediately following his Investiture, and the three-day tour with his wife in October – but commendable nevertheless when his extensive journeys abroad, his Service career and his personal holidays are taken into account.

Many of what were anticipated to be merely temporary interests in the Welsh way of life have become almost permanently established. His one-term secondment to the University College of Wales at Aberystwyth, shortly before his Investiture, prompted the College to award him an honorary Doctorate of Letters in

holds today. In addition he has been granted the Freedom of Cardiff and Montgomery.

As Colonel-in-Chief of the Royal Regiment of Wales since its foundation in 1969, he attended its inaugural ceremony in the grounds of Cardiff Castle in June of that year. He succeeded his father the Duke of Edinburgh as Colonel of the Welsh Guards in 1975, and attends the Trooping the Colour ceremony annually in that capacity.

Prince Charles understood and appreciated from the time of his earliest visits to Wales, the Welshman's fears of losing his identity while Wales was treated as a mere satellite of England. Many of those suspicions were expressed with horrifying abandon at the time of his Investiture and were reflected again in bomb scares during last October's tour. But his serious and genuine application to the care and stewardship of the

1972, and he perpetuated the relationship by becoming its Chancellor four years later. His chairmanship of the Prince of Wales' Committee for Wales, now twelve years old, was born out of a two-year post as Chairman of the Steering Committee for Wales in the "Countryside for 1970" Conference. His consuming passion for everything which obsesses the Welsh themselves has matured into patronage and presidencies in many fields.

He became Patron, for a period of five years, of the Wales in Bloom Campaign in 1970, President of the Welsh Environmental Foundation the following year, and President of the Welsh Committee of European Architectural Heritage Year in 1972. In 1974 he became Patron of the Friends of Brecon Cathedral, and in 1977 Patron of the Welsh Association of Male Voice Choirs – posts he still

Welsh heritage has done much to convince his people there that, while he is their Prince, their culture and ethnic values are in good hands.

APRIL 1982

Princess Margaret seems to experience the regular ill-fortune of being on duty inspecting military parades during particularly inclement weather. One remembers especially the occasion when she took the salute at an inspection of one of her regiments in Germany in 1979 with her eyes literally

streaming in the teeth of a bitter wind: so sharp that eventually she had to go inside the regiment's headquarters before the march-past was completed. She may have remembered that day on 8th April when she went to the Royal Military Academy at Sandhurst to review the Sovereign's parade on behalf of the Queen – who at that time was attending the annual service of the Royal Maundy at St David's Cathedral in Wales. Escorted by the College's new commandant, Major-General Geoffrey Howlett (left) she watched the impressive march-

past (above and left) and presented special awards (top left and centre right) to officer cadets. In all some 370 men were on parade, and for 142 of them this was the occasion of their formal commissioning into the British Army. A further 25 cadets from fifteen Commonwealth and other overseas countries also received their commissions.

Princess Margaret was well wrapped up against the icy wind,

stand-by to join the Task Force. Towards the end of March the Princess of Wales had visited Huddersfield (right) and Newcastle-upon-Tyne under a last-minute arrangement to see young people who were receiving cash aid from the Prince's Trust to improve their social surroundings or prospects. Prince Charles founded the Trust in 1976, after a three-year investigation based on the concern he felt about young people for whom a lack of purpose in life, brought on by social and economic difficulties, could lead to alienation. The

Prince had, on his own initiative, called a meeting of social workers and police represen-tatives at Buckingham Palace in December 1972 and from those tentative beginnings there now exists a full-time charity dispensing some £60,000 a year in grants.

On 30th March the Princess arrived back at Kings Cross Station (other pictures on this page) after opening St Gemma's Hospice in Leeds, with Prince Charles. She came back alone while the Prince went on to York to visit a Vikings Exhibition.

in her thick mink coat, but she was suffering from a heavy cold and sneezed several times during the parade. She also lost her handbag when it dropped from her hands and slipped under the table on the presentation podium.

The Falklands dispute was only a few days old and still a relatively delicate issue for public speaking. But Princess Margaret made a veiled reference to it, referring to "these troubled times." She told the newly-commissioned officers that their chosen career was "surely one of the most demanding and worthwhile professions" and she wished them every success in it. Coincidentally the band was provided by the Parachute Regiment which was then on

APRIL 1982

Following a full and enjoyable day with the Chinese community in Liverpool on 2nd April, the Princess of Wales was entertained by a less boisterous Japanese contingent the following week. On 7th April she visited Bridgend, in mid Glamorgan, to open what the Court Circular described that evening as "the new Picture Tube Plant of Sony (UK) Ltd." In less restrained and more modern language the factory complex produces television tubes, and its recent completion, in the heart of an area which

suggestion was taken up and both Sony and Wales have benefited from it. It is a sad reflection on the confidence of British industry in the principality, that Wales has the highest concentration of Japanese factories in the whole of Great Britain but for the Welsh, the point is of academic interest only.
The Princess arrived – hard on the heels of her husband, who only the day before had been visiting the Royal Mint just twenty miles away – in a Wessex helicopter of the Queen's Flight

tour of the factory. It didn't really go with her warm pink wool coat, but the Princess is nothing if not game for anything and after a time she looked as natural in them as if she had chosen them personally.
She was duly impressed both by the confident atmosphere of the factory and by the intricate workmanship which went into its products. "It is heartening in these times to see examples of expansion and success," she said, during her formal speech. "I will now watch television with new eyes, realising a little of

over the last few years has been heavily hit by swingeing redundancies in the steel and allied industries, brings the relief of employment for at least a hundred men and women, and the promise of better times ahead.
Sony was the first Japanese firm to establish a factory in Wales – indeed Prince Charles opened the first Sony factory, also in Glamorgan, back in 1974. That event had its origins in a meeting Prince Charles had had with Sony's President during his visit to Expo 70 in Tokyo four years earlier. He was told that Sony were looking for a European site for their next factory, and the Prince – conscious of his loyalties and obligations as Prince of Wales – suggested that it should be Wales. The

(top picture), after a bumpy journey which is reported to have left some of her staff looking and feeling just a little pale. She herself looked cheerful and in good spirits, with no sign of the depression which had prompted doctor's orders to take a holiday later that month, as she battled against the high winds (above) to reach the Sony building.
Within the factory gates of this £10 million plant, swathed in a tactful confection of national flags – the Union Jack, the red, white and green Welsh Flag and the Japanese national flag, the Princess was introduced to the firm's co-founder, Mr Masaru Ibuka, before being equipped with special glasses and a protective peaked cap (opposite page centre left) ready for her

what goes on within the set to achieve the final clear and vivid picture."

She left the factory with not only a smile but also a couple of cassette players for herself and Prince Charles, presented by the delighted and honoured Mr Ibuka. What a coincidence that the royal couple already had at least one Sony product already – the portable cassette players

given to them for their wedding by Sir Harry and Lady Secombe. On her way back to the helicopter she went off to meet some of the 2,000-strong crowd (left) and delighted them with her friendliness and patience. There was four-year-old Emma Thomas who, dressed in Welsh traditional costume, presented the Princess with a large bunch of daffodils and then asked to be

kissed – and, of course, was. There was Mrs Barbara Down who was able to present her with a good luck charm – containing a delicate silhouette of a mother-and-child. And the two young Woolls sisters, Larissa and Francesca, also in Welsh dress, were thrilled when the Princess' car was drawn up alongside them so that they could give her a hand-knitted baby coat.

Eventually, with a cheerful final wave (left) she took her leave of Bridgend on this her second visit to her new principality. It was essentially private and there were none of the intensely celebratory scenes which made the Prince and Princess' three-day tour of Wales in October such a memorable one. But it was her first solo engagement there, and one which manifested her growing confidence and her continuing enjoyment of royal life, despite the profound adjustments which her marriage to Prince Charles involved. This was to have been her last public engagement before the birth of her baby, but a few days later it was announced that another had been booked for 18th May.

APRIL 1982

The Queen and the Duke of Edinburgh, who had removed from Buckingham Palace to Windsor Castle on 28th March, followed the trend set that week by their son and daughter-in-law, and travelled to Wales to visit St David's and Haverfordwest on 8th April. The occasion of their visit was the annual service of the Royal Maundy, and only six months after receiving the Prince and Princess of Wales, St David's Cathedral was chosen as the venue for this ceremonial remembrance of the night

sovereign to carry out the office personally, and by the time the Hanoverians were established the act of humility had shrunk into the giving of food and clothing to the poor. In former days the bounty was as practical as any poor recipient could wish – throughout the centuries gifts of boiled beef, or shoulders of mutton, half sides of salmon, "jowles" of ling, white or pickled herrings, red sprats, "green fish or cod," and "six loaves of cheat bread," were distributed, along with dishes of claret, or "scales"

anniversary of the Battle of Tewkesbury. So in 1982, when St David's Cathedral celebrated its 800th anniversary, the Queen became the first sovereign ever to have distributed the Maundy in Wales.

St David's Cathedral (picture left), named after Wales' patron saint, completely dominates the small city below with its stout, impressive tower reaching almost 120 feet into the sky. It was constructed over a period of decades in the 12th and 13th centuries, from locally

before the Crucifixion when Christ washed the feet of His disciples as an act of humility which He commanded them to follow.

The command (Latin *mandatum*) is the essence of the ceremony, which affords parallels in several non-Anglican Christian Churches, but the practice of washing feet, which was performed from time to time by various monarchs, has long since been abandoned. King William III was probably the last

of wine, gallons of beer or small bowls of ale, lengths of woollen and linen cloth for essential clothing, together with pairs of stockings and shoes.

Today the ceremony is almost totally symbolic in that the recipients of the Royal Maundy receive purses containing fairly nominal amounts of money for clothing and food, together with specially minted Maundy money – sterling silver coins of four different face values: 4p, 3p, 2p and 1p, though with a silver content of much greater worth. But even this gift would not now be delivered by the Queen personally had it not been for her grandfather, King George V's decision to restore the tradition of the monarch's personal distribution, which had been in abeyance since the early eighteenth century. Indeed 1982 marked the fiftieth anniversary of that new tradition.

Until the early years of the present Queen's reign the Royal Maundy service, whether attended by the sovereign or

not, had been held in London for over two centuries. In 1957 the Queen decided to adapt the practice to take in provincial cathedral cities, St Albans being chosen that year. Many venues have been decided upon with reference to special anniversaries – thus Southwark Cathedral in 1955, to celebrate the Golden Jubilee of the Diocese, Rochester Cathedral in 1961, during its charter's 500th anniversary, and Tewkesbury Abbey in 1971 to mark the 500th

quarried sandstone, and its rich warm nave roofed in Irish oak is a fine example of its kind. The Queen and Prince Philip arrived at the Bell Tower, just within the Cathedral precincts, accompanied by the Bishop of St David's, the Right Reverend George Noakes, and descended a flight of stone steps – familiarly known as the 39 steps – into the Cathedral.

The service, in this building which was at one time a focal point for pilgrims from all over

Lord High Almoner, the Bishop of Rochester, distributed the gifts in two stages: in the first distribution 56 men and 56 women – the number of recipients of each sex increases each year with the Queen's age – received white and green purses respectively (left) each containing the clothing allowance. In the second, each person received a red and a white purse, one containing money for provisions, the other containing the Maundy coins with a total face value of 56p. After the service, the Queen and Prince Philip, both holding colourful nosegays of herbs and flowers – another tradition which dates back to the days of plague – made their way out of the cathedral with the Dean, the Very Reverend Lawrence Bowen, stopping to receive gifts from youngsters from the local primary schools who were among the large crowds gathered to see her.

Before returning to Heathrow Airport, the Queen and Prince Philip motored to Haverfordwest where they had lunch at the

Wales and the West Country, took its now hallowed and almost unchanging course. It began with the joyful hymn "Praise, my soul, the King of Heaven," sung with typical Welsh lyricism, and Psalm 138 was followed by one of the Maundy Service's usual anthems, "Lord, for thy tender mercies' Sake." The other two habitual anthems are Handel's Coronation anthem "Zadok the Priest" with its soaring narrative and intricate, fugal "Hallelujahs"

and "Amens," and Samuel Wesley's quiet, pastoral "Wash Me Thoroughly" recalling the holy example which has for so many years been absent from this annual service.

Prince Philip, as he always does, read one of the two lessons – the passage from St Matthew's gospel which contains the statement "In so much as ye have done it unto one of my brethren, ye have done it unto me."

The Queen, accompanied by the

Masonic Hall followed by a short walkabout in the town centre. Then it was back to Windsor where Easter celebrations awaited before the Queen's family dispersed again for their Summer term of duties. These would take the Queen herself off to Canada, Prince Philip and Princess Anne to the States, Prince Charles to France and, shortly, Prince Andrew off to the Falklands.

APRIL 1982

On 13th April, the Tuesday after Easter, Queen Elizabeth the Queen Mother left Clarence House for the Royal Albert Hall to attend a gala concert which, according to an understatement in the programme notes,

Philharmonic Orchestra, with whom he was to sing, and the Queen Mother's presence as Patron of the Orchestra at a concert staged as part of its National Appeal made the evening one of superlatives.

promised "to be one of London's musical events of the year." It was in fact the only scheduled appearance at a concert in the United Kingdom in 1982 of that superlative tenor opera singer Luciano Pavarotti. The occasion was all the more special because Pavarotti himself had substantially reduced his fees to help the Royal

Indeed, when a recording of the concert was shown on television a few days later, it was on the cards that opera had recruited a substantial number of new admirers.

At 47, Pavarotti has acquired every tribute the opera world could possibly heap on one man. For a singer whose professional début did not occur until the age of 26, it must be praise indeed to be commended for having a voice which in various ways can be likened to Caruso's, Gigli's or Björling's. He first performed in England in 1962 – at Covent Garden, which occupies a very important place in the milestone history of his career.

The programme was by modern standards a colossal one, with four orchestral pieces and seven operatic arias including three by Verdi and two by Puccini, and after the concert Pavarotti was introduced to the Queen Mother (above left). Opera is not thought to be the Queen Mother's listening forte though she has had an accomplished ear for music since childhood, and when young sang "very prettily," according to her music mistress. But it is inconceivable that Pavarotti's performance did less than rivet her – these pictures show her looking as fresh as a daisy, lively and with that famous wagging finger (opposite page bottom left) in animated conversation with the celebrity whose singing she unreservedly enjoyed. For a great-grandmother striding confidently towards her 82nd birthday, she looked a picture of appreciation, was charmed by Pavarotti's chivalrous gestures – reminiscent of some Renaissance

established and she may have passed a few tips on. Financially the concert was a massive success, and the Royal Philharmonic will have been pleased and thankful for that. The box office takings showed the largest amount their performances had ever drawn at any concert hall anywhere in the

world – almost £150,000. For an organisation which at some of its concerts pays back to the Government in VAT more than it receives in grants, that must be compensation enough, but it was also satisfying to know that this was not an occasion solely for the wealthy. Of the 6,000 tickets sold, 3,500 were available at £15 or less, including 1,000 student tickets at only £2.50 each. The result was the largest "live" audience ever to hear Pavarotti in the UK, and every one of them, like the Queen Mother, surely satisfied with the exquisite performance of a man who according to the title of one of his own records is "King of the High C's."

gallant (far right), and as thrilled as Pavarotti was honoured by the presentation to her of one of his eight records currently available (above right). And did they, perhaps for a few brief moments, exchange the latest gossip on the equestrian scene? Pavarotti's interest in horse racing and thoroughbred breeding is as recent as the Queen Mother's is well

APRIL 1982

The thirty-first Badminton Three-day Event – it has been held every year since its inauguration in 1949 – got underway in the grounds of the Duke of Beaufort's Gloucestershire mansion on 15th April. This prestigious, well-attended and thorough test of all-round horsemanship, with the Whitbread Trophy and a prize of £3,000 for the winner, attracted a gate of almost 200,000 people, and a field of seventy-nine competitors. Among them were twenty initiates aged less than 25, as well as the much more seasoned campaigners, Princess Anne (below) and her husband Captain Mark Phillips (right).

Badminton mount, Classic Lines, is being prepared. The dressage took up two days of the Badminton programme, and both Princess Anne (No 72) and Captain Phillips (No 83) competed on the second day. Both had submitted their horses to the usual veterinary inspection on the evening of the 14th April, and each horse was declared sound. But despite this and the opportunities for practice runs (below and right) the previous day, Classic Lines conceded 60.6 penalty points in the dressage, leaving Captain Phillips well down the field. Princess Anne, who had not competed at Badminton since 1979, fared rather better with a

Princess Anne (seen above riding the Queen's horse Stevie B in the first phase of the competition, the dressage, on 16th April) has never yet won at Badminton, but Captain Phillips, like Lucinda Prior-Palmer-Green who won in 1973, 1976, 1977 and 1979, has run out victor on a record four different occasions – in 1971 and 1972 on

his horse Great Ovation, in 1974 on the Queen's horse Columbus, and in 1981 on Lincoln, a horse sponsored by Range Rover Team, as part of the deal he made with Land Rover Ltd in 1980. The sponsorship, arranged amid considerable public criticism, has brought Captain Phillips in excess of £75,000, including over £10,000 in prize

money – mostly from his tally of sixteen victories in 1981. Shortly before Badminton it was announced that the sponsoring partnership would be continued until December 1983, with an option to extend for two further years. This will take Captain Phillips into the reckoning for the 1984 Olympics at Los Angeles, an event for which his

final total of 58.2 penalties. The following day, fortunes were quite dramatically reversed. Captain Phillips, who later declared that he was "thrilled with Classic Lines' performance in the dressage and cross-country," came home with a clear round in the cross country phase – recognised as one of the most gruelling of its kind in

Europe, with its total of 32 obstacles comprising steps, ditches, hedges, rails, fences, ski-jumps and lakes. This performance lifted him to eventual 14th place, two places short of the entitlement to the smallest prize of £125. Princess Anne did not, however, have such a good day. She had already had one of her regular altercations with the army of photographers who have followed her equestrian career with unstinting interest, when her exasperation reached breaking point the previous day. "Why don't you all grow up," she told them. "You've been taking the same pictures of me every day for three days. Why

don't you naff off. Go on, shove off." In no mood to do either, the photographers were waiting for her at the eighteenth fence in the cross country – the upturned punt barring entry into the lake. This is usually the spot where her husband comes a cropper, but this time Stevie B's hooves clipped the punt and Princess

for them both. In June 1981 Mark had been in the winning British team at the European championships at Hooge Mierde in Holland and was joined by Princess Anne at the Burghley Horse Trials in September – she won there in 1971 to take the European Championship that year. Unfortunately both of them landed in water ditches during the cross country, and came away unplaced.

October was another bad month: although Captain Phillips won £1,500 prize money at Wylye Horse Trials near Salisbury, Princess Anne was nearly knocked down by another rider when she was helping to rebuild one of the fallen fences. Later that month Mark went to

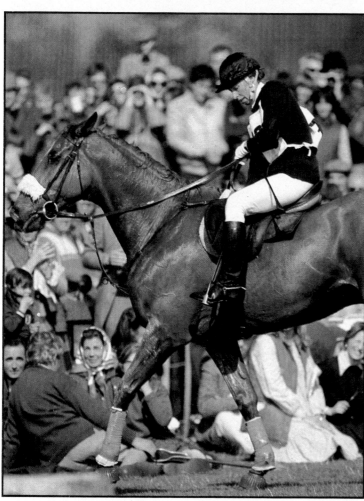

Anne, unable to control his imbalance, nosedived with him into the lake (opposite page). She retrieved the horse and paddled out of the lake, her white nylon breeches transparent and her riding boots full of water. Surprisingly cheerful – or at least philosophical (top right) – she decided to

retire from the event and trotted off back to the stables, though not before she had cast a final malediction the way of the photographers. "I hope you're all happy. You've got what you wanted now."

So ended the Phillipses twelfth Badminton challenge, in what had been a busy equestrian year

compete in Australia, where he found considerably more interest being shown in the rumours of a rift in his marriage. In a radio interview, for which he was said to have asked a fee of £6,000, he faced up to the long-running stories of a liaison between him and former BBC newsreader Angela Rippon, who had been commissioned to write a book called "Mark Phillips, The Man and His Horses" – which, incidentally she launched at Badminton on 15th April. He denied any romance, saying that he and Princess Anne had got to know Miss Rippon very well – "after all, it takes a long time to write a book. Princess Anne and

I are not at all happy about the rumours. Nor was Miss Rippon – she too is happily married." The same month brought an astonishing statement from Councillor Jim Spencer, a Liberal member of Otley Town Council in West Yorkshire who, in a debate about the local horse-riding fraternity, protested that "horses are ridden by base and coarse people like Princess Anne." Just a joke, he said afterwards.

Captain Phillips' luck failed to improve over the New Year. He had to admit that he needed a complete break from horses after a heavy 18-month

schedule. He had taken an enforced rest when his back began to play up in November, and decided to prolong it over Christmas. He then found himself a stone and a half overweight as his training deadline approached and had to work hard to get himself in trim again.

In January he was unable to get from Gatcombe to Upminster where he was due to compete in the Martell Cognac Championships; heavy snow delayed his train from Stroud, and attempts to charter a helicopter failed. By February he was campaigning to save Aintree, now in one of its recurring death throes; he had jumped the course back in 1979 and thought it "one of the greatest experiences of my life: it would be a tragic loss."

March saw both him and Princess Anne back in the saddle with a vengeance: at Crookham Horse Trials he rode his "second" horse Blizzard II,

while she competed on her younger horse Soul Song. They both competed later at Downlands Horse Trials near Liphook, and Mark was out again at Wendover Horse Trials towards the end of the month. And, as a postscript to Badminton, Princess Anne rode Soul Song at Hagley Horse Trials in Worcestershire in April. He refused at the water ditch, and she fell in. Plus ça change ...

Princess Anne has long been branded the black sheep of the Royal Family, and often without the tolerant endearments which that expression often connotes.

Her frequent brushes with the Press – usually at some equestrian event – and the Press' own retaliatory sarcasm against her whenever she uses the word "one" to mean "I" or "me," has brought the Princess' public image into what at one stage looked like irretrievable disfavour.

One accusation frequently levelled against her is that she unnecessarily distances herself from the Press and her public. Yet she is the best known of all the Queen's children in the sense that she has invited a considerable amount of publicity into her activities both public and private. Ever since the

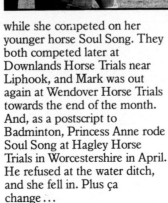

rather disastrous pre-wedding interview she and Captain Phillips gave in November 1973 for transmission by both television corporations – "It was a night to turn monarchists into republicans and republicans into monarchists," said one critic – interviews and filming facilities have been given regularly in and around Oak Grove House at Sandhurst, and Gatcombe Park. As a result, we have enjoyed in particular a unique insight into the way the Princess and her husband throw themselves into their consuming equestrian pastimes.

Only rarely has the Princess spoken in detail of her public life – how she approaches it, how important she feels it is, what she gets out of it. That was partly remedied when she was interviewed in December 1981 for the ITV programme "Princess Anne, Her Working Life." In it she envisaged that her

children would be free to pursue their careers without having to perform official duties. She cited Princess Margaret's children as examples, but she might more aptly have chosen the family of her great-aunt, the late Princess Royal. Her brothers produced families who answered the royal call, but her own sons, Lord Harewood and Mr Gerald Lascelles, are conveniently off the royal hook.

As if to demonstrate that he has no intention of being very royal, Princess Anne's son Peter ran amok at Badminton, giving the crowds more entertainment than they had paid to see. Finding a

kindred spirit in 10-year-old Alexander Lochore, whose father is a friend of Princess Anne, he began racing round the collecting ring, squealing and shouting as he darted between his mother's legs, swinging round them and throwing both parents off balance with some pretty physical charges. Captain

Phillips remonstrated (opposite page right), so did Princess Anne, but Peter was in too boisterous a mood to take the hint. Eventually, Princess Anne took him off (above) to one of her grooms and he was led, protesting, out of the compound.

APRIL 1982

Two of the most recent royal regulars at Badminton are Prince Michael and Princess Michael of Kent, seen here on 17th April enjoying the thrills and spills of the cross country Speed and Endurance Test, as well as a few much more personal moments (bottom picture and opposite page extreme right). Their attendance each year (including last year, only days before the Princess gave birth to her second child) is no mere social appearance. Both share wide equestrian interests. Prince Michael often goes hunting, though not always with satisfactory results: in October 1981 he was one of a succession of riders who were thrown from their horses at a Meet of the Quorn in Leicestershire. Princess Michael regularly supports equestrian events close to their home at Nether Lypiatt in Gloucestershire, such as the point-to-point at Didmarton which she attended in March, just before this year's Badminton.

end of March, to inspect Britain's next entry for the Americas Cup, and Princess Michael was invited to name the £300,000 yacht 'Victory.'
At the other extreme of their combined interests is their penchant for the arts. Like her talented mother-in-law, Princess Marina, Princess Michael paints, though "very badly" she admits, "in water colours," preferring to

fare. This film, starring Jeremy Irons, was one of three official British entries this year, and Prince Michael backed it financially. Among the films and plays Prince and Princess Michael saw during the year were "The Little Foxes" in March, when they met Elizabeth Taylor; the charity premiere of

The horse world forms only part of the royal couple's sporting interests. Despite the accident twelve years ago which almost killed him, Prince Michael has never lost his enthusiasm for bobsleighing. As President of the British Bobsleigh Association he agreed to open the Thorpe Training Run for bobsleigh practice in Chertsey in September 1981, and the following January visited the British team at St Moritz as they trained for their annual assault on the World Championships. Prince Michael's interest in sailing took him to Cowes at the

paint still lifes and flowers: "I don't paint as well as Princess Marina did and feel I have a lot to live up to." Her ambition is to have one of her works accepted by the Society of Women Artists, whose annual exhibition she opened at the Mall Galleries in February.
The cinema and theatre have Prince Michael's support: he visited the Cannes Film Festival in May specifically to see how the film "Moonlighting" would

"On Golden Pond" at the Empire Leicester Square, and the new £1½ million production of "The Pirates of Penzance" at the Savoy.
Rumour had it that the Prince and Princess could even be going into television, with Prince Michael as non-executive director of the television company AMTV and his wife as a breakfast television presenter. Even their private secretary was quoted as saying, "Indeed why

not? It's an intriguing suggestion." But all is quiet on that front at present: perhaps Princess Michael is too busy finishing her book on Elizabeth of Bohemia – the Winter Queen, daughter of our own King James I and a direct ancestress of the House of Windsor.

It was during a visit to Holland to research for the book that, on 16th February, Princess Michael was taken ill with severe abdominal pains. She was rushed off to King Edward VII Hospital for Officers in Marylebone, where two days of

catch up on her work. And work, which during the year has taken her and Prince Michael to Belize to represent the Queen at independence in September 1981, and as close to home as Westminster Abbey for the Children of Courage awards in December, seems to be varied, interesting and enjoyable. Certainly few have taken up the royal role with as much unashamed gusto as has Princess Michael, with her regal bearing, superbly chosen wardrobe, glittering jewels and expansive gestures. David Bailey's official photograph of

examination and tests amid rumours that she was pregnant or had suffered a miscarriage, showed that her gall bladder was the cause of the trouble. Prince Michael was at her bedside for most of this worrying time, and even brought their two children to see their mother who "was missing them, and the doctors thought it would be a tonic for her." Lord Frederick looked a picture in his piped jacket and knickerbockers. After an operation for the removal of her gall bladder, Princess Michael emerged from hospital "feeling fine" on 1st March, and went back to Kensington Palace to

her in a rich blue gown with extravagant ruffles and puffed sleeves was a classic of royal portraiture, and the image of one who revels in her new role was well captured.

Unfortunately the Princess is not without her critics. One newspaper columnist accused her of commercialising her job; others fondly supposed that her sheer enjoyment of it has upstaged the likes of Princess Margaret and even the Princess of Wales. But she remains unimpressed and is rightly content to continue in her own enthusiastic way.

APRIL 1982

The Queen Mother, who has attended Badminton almost invariably since 1949, was as usual much in evidence, being ferried from one obstacle to another as she watched the competitors in the cross country event. In the absence of the Queen and Prince Philip, who were in Canada, the Queen Mother was escorted by the Duke of Beaufort (right and below right) who hosted the entire event. He is exactly four months older than the Queen Mother, to whom he is, by marriage, a first cousin: Queen Mary, who spent the years of the

Second World War at Badminton, was aunt to the 85-year-old Duchess of Beaufort. On the concluding day of Badminton, Sunday 18th April, the Queen Mother was escorted by Prince Edward to Morning Service at Badminton's small village church (above and far right). The previous day Prince Edward had taken the opportunity to try out part of the course. Like Princess Anne, he too came to verbal blows with photographers desperate to obtain their pictures. 'Stop running after me like a bunch of idiots,' he shouted at them. 'You're frightening my horse.' Badminton was Prince Edward's last respite, save for a brief return to Windsor for the Horse Trials in May, from his busy final few months at Gordonstoun. Leaving for his last term on 21st April – his mother's 56th birthday – he was appointed Guardian (or Head Boy) of the School, and when he left on 11th July, a day marked by a visit

join the Royal Marines and on 17th May he began a three-day officer assessment course at their Commando Training Centre at Lympstone, Devon. Here he observed and was briefed about its activities, and was put through his paces in a preliminary test of his suitability. He found himself running up a 6-foot wall, climbing up rope

from the Queen, his headmaster, Mr Michael Mavor, said he had been a very good all rounder. Events proved him to be more than that. After a short period of modest reticence, Buckingham Palace announced in the middle of August that the Queen's youngest son had emerged as the most academically talented. He passed all his 'A' levels at Gordonstoun with flying colours,

gaining a distinctive 'S' level pass in one of his three subjects. So his temporary post as housemaster at Wanganui begins auspiciously.
But Prince Edward was already looking beyond that, and into the prospects of a Service career in the footsteps of his two elder brothers.
During the term it was announced that he intended to

nets, crawling through pipes and launching himself, Tarzan-style, from a 50-foot-high tower, finishing up with a 'very good' official rating – and a slight nosebleed. If, after this, he still wants to go ahead and is accepted, he will join the Marines in September 1983, when his two-term stay at Wanganui's School in New Zealand is completed.

APRIL 1982

The Queen's absence from Badminton was only her second since the event began, the last time being after the birth of Prince Edward in 1964. It was ironic that after more than half a century's wrangling over the most effective and acceptable way to sever the last colonial link between Britain and Canada, the formal ceremony to despatch the quarrel should have been so hastily organised that the Queen's constitutional presence in Canada should be necessary on the very dates of the one country event she has so loyally

attended since before her accession.

The Duke of Beaufort was naturally very disappointed – so the Duchess confirmed, adding, "and I know the Queen is too." Colonel Frank Weldon, Director of the Horse Trials, went one better and disclosed that the Queen, whose job in Canada he called "dreary and unpleasant," had written to the Duke, regretting her absence, saying that she would have liked the Canadian ceremony to have been postponed till after Badminton and that she had tried to get the dates changed so that she could attend both. An almighty row broke out in the Badminton camp over the Colonel's revelation, while Buckingham Palace tried to keep a delicate neutrality.

It was nothing like the row that awaited the Queen when she arrived in Ottawa (above right), having travelled in a Canadian Armed Forces Boeing 707 (top right) from Heathrow on 15th April. (Unusually, she stepped out of the aircraft in the same outfit as she had entered it. She usually changes en route). For as she was being introduced by Governor-General Ed Schreyer (above, far right) to a line of dignitaries, inspecting the guard of honour (opposite page, left centre) and signing the VIP's Visitors Book (opposite page

bottom left), the Premier of the separatist Quebec provincial government, René Levesque, was finalising plans for half a dozen protest meetings, and a boycott of the official ceremony at which Canada would assume full responsibility for her own constitution. Monsieur Levesque, the man who achieved fleeting notoriety a few years back for holding a lighted cigarette as the Queen was being officially introduced to him, said: "It's crazy for the Queen to come here. We refuse to accept her bringing us our symbolic

independence," and his political intransigence on this occasion was partly responsible for the massive security which surrounded the Queen during her visit.

The issue which prompted the Queen's visit has loomed large in Canada's history. Anti-colonial rebellions in Canada in 1837 had led, thirty years later, to the British North America Act, which placed the internal affairs of the Canadian confederation of provinces within their own power, while constitutional and foreign affairs were reserved to

Great Britain. A gentle process of transferring these reserved powers followed, and by the time of the Imperial Conference of 1926 only constitutional sovereignty remained seriously at issue. By the Statute of Westminster of 1931, the British Parliament lost the power to make any legislation on behalf· of Canada, or indeed of any other Dominion. Formal approval by Britain of Canadian laws amending its constitution was retained, and it was this which proved a sticking point, not so much between Canada

and embittered Eskimos whose claims, if they went unrecognised or merely ignored, might swell the ranks of the disaffected. Though at no time during the Queen's four-day visit could these considerations have been far from her mind, she looked her usual composed and welcoming self as, on 16th April, she entertained guests at a State reception and banquet at the Governor-General's residence (overleaf). Prince Philip, who had been unable to travel with her the previous day because of an official

and Britain but between the English and French-speaking populations of Canada. Although, under the new Constitution Act of 1982, all restrictions, whether substantive or merely formal, on the rights of Canadians to legislate for themselves were removed, the substitution of the new charter of rights, both human and political, was seen by the separatists as giving perpetual power to the English-speaking majority. Monsieur Levesque had secured the support of dispossessed Canadian Indians

engagement in Berkshire – taking the Salute at a passing out parade of REME Officers at the Princess Marina College, Berkshire – arrived in Ottawa in time to join her for this occasion (left and above left). The Queen was wearing the shimmering, lattice-patterned evening dress she had worn the previous month at the State banquet she gave at Buckingham Palace for the Sultan of Oman, with her Canadian orders in place of her more usual personal family orders. She also sported a matching combination of diamond and ruby jewellery – the necklace which she has worn on State occasions since her State Visit to Western Germany in 1965 and the tiara which she had had made up from her own collection of stones for the visit to Windsor by the President of Mexico in 1973, and which has been her particular favourite on previous visits to Canada. Beneath portraits of previous

APRIL 1982

Governors-General of Canada, the Queen and Prince Philip, accompanied by the present Governor-General and his wife (bottom left), welcomed a long succession of official and diplomatic guests, among whom was the British Shadow Foreign Minister, former Prime Minister Edinburgh's Award. A hundred young achievers were accordingly presented at Rideau Hall on 16th April. The following day the Queen presided at the swearing-in of eleven new members of the Privy Council – including all the provincial premiers save intact, while the Commons and Senate chambers were completely rebuilt in the more austere, less florid style of post-War years. And that evening, her last of the visit, she attended a gala concert at the National Arts Centre as well as a dinner given in her honour by the Canadian Prime Minister, Pierre Trudeau (opposite page, below right and bottom pictures).

The central ceremony of the visit and the signing of the Proclamation giving effect to the new Act, took place in weather as variable as its political fortunes in the decades before its

Mr James Callaghan (top right).

The banquet was one of several official engagements which kept the Queen and Prince Philip well occupied throughout their stay in Canada as part of the ceremonial ancillary to the handing over of the country's constitution. Prince Philip had already attended one of his frequent receptions at which he awards Certificates of Achievement to winners at Gold Standard of the Duke of Monsieur Levesque – in a ceremony in the Privy Council chamber of the Canadian Parliament.

She also inaugurated the East Block of the legislative complex, newly renovated in a four-year-long project, in keeping with the original mid-Victorian character of the building as a whole – the West Block has been changed substantially through the years, and the Centre Block was destroyed by fire in 1916, leaving only the Parliamentary Library

ultimate agreement on 5th November 1981. As if to prophesy an age of uncertainty, brilliant sunshine alternated with tremendously heavy downpours of rain as the Royal Standard broke over the rambling, Gothic Parliament building and fluttered wildly atop the 220 foot high Peace Tower. A crowd of 50,000 stood on and around the vast lawns in front of it, unfurling umbrellas or hastily putting on anoraks and cagoules, while 24 million people watching television more comfortably at home awaited the arrival of the Queen.

There was little in the way of preliminary activity. In the space of an hour before the official ceremony, a succession of distinguished guests arrived at the Parliament building, while

the waiting crowds were entertained by a programme of music and song from the Mount Royal Children's Choir from Calgary, "Les Alino" from Moncton, New Brunswick and the Central Band of the Canadian Forces. Ultimately, ten minutes before the Queen, Mr Trudeau arrived, smiling with the satisfaction of achievement but conscious of the significance of the solemn and historic occasion to follow, and was greeted by Canada's Secretary of State. Five minutes later the Governor-General arrived and proceeded to the saluting base to receive an official vice-regal salute and to greet the Queen. She and Prince Philip arrived at Parliament Hill in a hundred-year-old State Landau drawn by four black horses, and escorted

APRIL 1982

by 47 scarlet-jacketed officers of the Royal Canadian Mounted Police, also on shining black horses. The Queen wore a blue woollen coat and matching hat and, for the ceremony itself, added two of her Canadian orders. Prince Philip looked dapper and impressive, as usual on such occasions, if less familiar in the uniform of the Royal Canadian Regiment of which he is Colonel. As they alighted from their carriage, a 21-gun salute, fired by the 30th Canadian Field Regiment, boomed from across the Ottawa River, while the band of the Royal 22nd Regiment, comprising mostly French-speaking soldiers, struck up with the National Anthem.

Overhead a noisy but impressive flypast by two squadrons of the Canadian Air Force completed the ceremonial salute as the Queen began a short inspection of the Guard of Honour provided by the Royal 22nd Regiment's 3rd Battalion. This completed, its band played the Canadian anthem "O Canada"

sovereignty." He was anxious to lay none of the blame for the decades-long delay at Britain's feet and willingly acknowledged that the rump of the British connection had lasted so unconscionably long for no better reason than that no-one could agree how best to have the last vestiges of power transferred

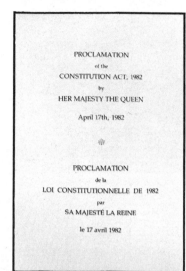

PROCLAMATION
of the
CONSTITUTION ACT, 1982
by
HER MAJESTY THE QUEEN

April 17th, 1982

PROCLAMATION
de la
LOI CONSTITUTIONNELLE DE 1982
par
SA MAJESTÉ LA REINE

le 17 avril 1982

and the crowds momentarily fell emotionally silent. But not for long. To frantic cheers from crowds up to ten deep in places, the royal couple were led by Mr Trudeau to a specially constructed dais (seen above right), ablaze with red carpet and plush thrones, for the open-air signing ceremony.

In a brief foreword, the Secretary of State explained the ceremony, its background, its purpose and its procedure. Mr Trudeau then stood to deliver his own address, rejoicing, though respectfully that "The Constitution has at last come home," and that "Today at long last, Canada has acquired full and complete

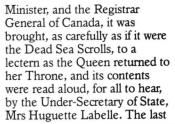

Minister, and the Registrar General of Canada, it was brought, as carefully as if it were the Dead Sea Scrolls, to a lectern as the Queen returned to her Throne, and its contents were read aloud, for all to hear, by the Under-Secretary of State, Mrs Huguette Labelle. The last

into Canadian hands. "This is the last colonial link with Britain," he continued; "the end of a long winter, the breaking up of the ice-jams and the beginning of a new Spring."

The Proclamation putting the new measure into effect was then brought to the Queen who, with her Canadian Prime Minister, proceeded to a polished table for the signing ceremony. She was the first to put her pen to it, signing 'Elizabeth R' in a script so unusually large for her that historians might have been reminded of John Hancock, who signed his name to the American Declaration of Independence deliberately grandly, so that, as he said, "King George can read it without having to put on his spectacles."
After the document had been additionally signed by the Prime

word lay with the Queen. There was a nine-jet fly-past from the Canadian Armed Forces' precision squadron 'The Snowbirds,' but the noise they made was nothing to the enormous thunderclap which coincided with the Queen's first words and preceded another torrential helping of rain. The Queen ventured no interpretation of this celestial signal, in jest or otherwise, but

spoke, in oblique references to the separatists, about the "differences and rivalries which have been part of Canada's history, and will probably always exist in such a vast and vigorous land." More specifically, she continued: "Although we regret the absence of its Premier, it is right to associate the people of Quebec with this celebration, because without them Canada would not be what she it today." So Great Britain's last hold on Canada's independence had been yielded up with good grace, and the old Dominion's "new Spring" had begun joyfully. And still the rain came down. It continued throughout the royal walkabout, in which the Queen held her own large black umbrella as she met a few of the enormous crowd of spectators, many of whom carried banners proclaiming 'God Save Canada,' or 'Proud to be Canadian' or 'Long Live the Queen . . . and Trudeau Too.' Meanwhile, the resilient Monsieur Levesque

watched with considerable satisfaction the progress of his own protest rallies in Montreal. A 15,000 audience, somewhat fewer than expected, but sizeable enough considering the weather, turned up in Jeanne Mance Park, waving anti-royalist banners, protesting about the presence of a 'foreign monarch' in the country, and shouting 'Elizabeth go home.'

M. Levesque, speaking beneath flags quartered with the old French Valois fleur-de-lys, reminded his listeners that he represented some 25% of Canada's twenty-five million population, and said that Quebec should reject the new deal with Britain because it would weaken the province by increasing the powers of the predominantly English-speaking central government. He spoke of Quebec's destiny as a nation in itself, but emphasised that the Quebecois should try to realise that destiny within the political process and 'without hostility.' Smaller, but significant rallies were held in four other Quebec towns.

For the majority, there was no underestimating the feeling of national pride which accompanied the staid, formal,

royal ceremony. 'Constitution Finally Home' proclaimed the Quebec Sunday Express in letters an inch and a half high, and 'Emotional Outburst Greets Constitution's Homecoming,' in a headline to an article speaking of 'the dawning of a new era of history.' It was without doubt an historic occasion unprecedented in living memory, and for most a triumphant, if long delayed, sequel to the story begun by the four million Canadians who became Dominion citizens in 1867.

The rain had stopped, but the wind was just as mischievous as, on 18th April, the Queen took her leave of a Canada with a newly-won status. Returning to the airport where she had landed three days earlier, she prepared to board the same aircraft for her flight back to London. Prince Philip was with her but only to the bottom of the aircraft steps. He was on his way to America, where he would be piloting the new Rolls-Royce powered

Boeing 757 jetliner, recently completed and tested in Seattle. So there was a swift but unprecedented public kiss (left) as she went her way and, fifteen minutes later, he went his. Both were back home in time for the Queen's 56th birthday three days later, in the familiar setting of Windsor Castle and in the company of members of the Royal Family. But the Prince and Princess of Wales were holidaying in the Scillies, and Prince Andrew was heading for the South Atlantic to prepare for a confrontation in which, ironically, Britain was seeking to regain control of the tiny, long-treasured possession of the Falkland Islands, having just ceded power, peacefully and willingly, to the vast former dominion of Canada.

APRIL 1982

Any holiday is worth the taking but when you can justify one on doctor's orders – even for only four days and then not entirely untrammelled by reminders of the daily round – there is something furtively pleasurable about it all. So the Princess of Wales must have felt when, at the end of March, after a run of public appearances that did little for her easy-going reputation, she was ordered to take a break away from it all. And as with the holiday in the Bahamas, news of the royal destination soon leaked out.

It was to be St Mary's, the largest of the six main Scilly Isles and capital of the scores of islands large and small, and innumerable rocks and ledges which make up this maritime haven of benign climate and gorgeous flowers which would do any Mediterranean coast proud – and all less than forty miles from Land's End. Needless to say, the Scillonians were beside themselves, in their

own quiet way, with excitement at the news. The Scillies are part of the Duchy of Cornwall and as Prince Charles was to bring his wife there for the first time, the islanders felt the need to be very protective towards their new landlady.

The promise of protection turned to threat when it was known that a sizeable contingent of journalists was to be allowed onto the islands. Any capers remotely resembling the business on Eleuthera would be punished by a ducking in the suitably icy waters of the Atlantic, and all royal public appearances were to be recorded

with due respect for law and order. As one official said: "Today we've got the gear to blast any reporter off his bike at two miles." And one regular weekender, setting off from Bournemouth to spend his Easter holiday on St Mary's said he would personally "kick out anyone who tried to make a mess of my landlord's holiday." There is little height to be found on the Scillies. None of the islands reaches more than 150 feet above sea level, but on the only respectably rising ground of St Mary's sits the comparatively newly-built bungalow "Tamarisk" which has been the Prince of Wales' personal holiday home since the early 1970's. Not that he has visited it much: he spent an early private holiday there in 1973, and stayed there again during a semi-official visit three years later. Despite its relative eminence – from its white-painted window niches you can see both the harbour and clusters of outlying islets – it

April when the Prince and Princess arrived, forty minutes late, at St Mary's Airport in a Wessex helicopter piloted by the Prince himself. A hundred and fifty photographers and reporters recorded every step of their disembarkation and followed their Land Rover as it sped round the perimeter road, stopping only, at the Princess' request, to acknowledge a greeting from a 4-year-old girl who handed a bunch of flowers to her through the window. They went on their way to a reception at the Town Hall, where 250 guests were waiting, every minute precious as the vehicle waltzed through the winding lanes in an attempt to make up for lost time.

Both Press and people were able to savour the royal visit at much greater leisure when, that evening, the Prince and Princess came back into the centre of St Mary's (previous page and this page) for a delightfully

nestles inconspicuously behind several less attractive buildings used as Duchy of Cornwall offices, its red-tiled roof peeping above late eighteenth century fortifications built to fend off the parvenu Napoleon. Tamarisk's housekeeper, Miss Elsie Hall, a guest at the Royal Wedding and at the Prince and Princess of Wales' Highgrove garden party given in 1981 for Duchy staff, promised them a pleasant, quiet holiday, assuring them that St Mary's was one of the few places where "anyone as well known as the Prince can stay without being bothered by sightseers." It wasn't quite like that on 20th

casual walkabout. The Princess had changed from her green sailor-boy collared dress she had worn for her arrival, to a summery maternity frock of blue with white polka dots – one of the first of many lightweight dresses she was to wear in the last two months of her pregnancy. Through the bunting-bedecked streets the royal progress was as slow – for the bodyguards a trifle too slow – as the morning arrival had been hurried. Someone who had presumably had the foresight to bring a stopwatch and a calculator with him reported that the royal couple took 22 minutes to walk a hundred yards and that the Princess alone collected 74 posies in the attempt. It was a believable mathematical summary. The Prince chatted amiably to the locals, pumping them with all manner of questions, including one about the water supply, and venturing to imagine that any

the cordon designed to separate royalty and commoners (below left), much to the delight of the thousands who filled the street to see her.

As the royal couple returned to their bungalow, police divers were checking the two boats which the Prince and Princess would be using for their next

landed when conquering the Scillies in 938 and where he established the first monastery. The monastery, along with all the islands, was handed over to Tavistock Abbey in Henry I's reign a century and a half later and reverted to the Crown after the dissolution of the monasteries under Henry VIII.

Queen Elizabeth I commenced a four-centuries-long succession of leases of the islands, which continues today – Tresco is tenanted to Mr Robert Dorrien Smith whose boat *Melledgan* was to take his royal landlords from St Mary's.

Of the four days of their visit this was to be the most private, Tresco's population of 150 souls being the only witnesses to its events. The island was completely closed to tourists and Mr Dorrien Smith's boat was the only one plying to and from St Mary's, the normal public ferrying service having been suspended for the day. As the Prince and Princess travelled from their holiday retreat to St Mary's harbour where, after meeting the crew of the *Melledgan* (pictures overleaf), they were assisted into the boat, the hundred who saw them off would be the last substantial crowds they would see that day.

problems would be overcome as "I don't suppose there are any dirty people in such a charming town as this." The Princess meanwhile made for her favourite audiences: young children, each of who seemed to be waving a flag, holding a bunch of flowers or both (bottom picture) and pensioners whom in one instance she approached by ducking under

day's outing. Mindful of the tragedy which overtook Lord Mountbatten almost three years earlier, they were taking no last-minute chances, and indeed the entire complement of the Devon and Cornwall police diving team were in St Mary's harbour that night.

The following day's destination was Tresco, the island upon which King Athelstan's men first

The short journey to Tresco took them within sight of the places where, despite an abundance of lighthouses on the islands, ships were once blown to their doom in the teeth of the frequent storms which lash the Scillies and make them such a notorious navigational hazard. One of the most famous

shipwrecks from which the islanders once derived a continuing source of wealth was the *Association,* one of three ships of Sir Cloudesley Shovel's fleet which foundered in 1707 with the loss of 2,000 men. Happily Prince Charles' less spectacular transport fared better and he and his wife landed on Tresco well in time for lunch. Less happily, the Princess began to feel slightly sea-sick and was only too pleased to put her feet on terra firma.

The couple toured the ancient ruins of Tresco Abbey and visited the almost fabled Abbey gardens, unique in Britain for their wealth of subtropical plants. The gardens were established in 1834 by Augustus John Smith, the lessee of the islands, whose family tenanted it as Lords Proprietor of the Isles for three quarters of a century. Smith planted a complex of trees to act as a shelter from the

worst of a changeable weather pattern, and the equable and often humid climate, which averages 60°C in the summer and well over 40°C in winter, was available for the growth of acacia, veronica, fuchsia, pelargonium and cineraria, as well as Australian ferns, South African mesembryanthemum and Mexican cacti.

The Prince and Princess had timed their holiday well, for the Abbey's vast display of deep yellow daffodils, descendants of those planted in the ground by the pre-Reformation monks, were in their prime, along with narcissi and the deep blues of late irises.

After a tour of the island, they returned to St Mary's where Prince Charles was hailed by the crew of an Irish yacht moored in the harbour. They invited him aboard, promising him an abundance of whisky if he joined them. "I'll take you up on that," answered Prince Charles, and three hours later did so, leaving

his wife at home nursing the aftermath of her queasiness. She had recovered by next morning and was wearing another flowing blue maternity dress when she accompanied Prince Charles to a lunch he was giving for the staff and tenants of the Duchy. Afterwards the royal couple met the kitchen staff who had prepared the meal, and who included Mrs Jacqueline Pritchard with her five-month-old baby Helen. The baby gripped the Princess' finger in her hand; the Princess tickled

her toes and spoke with mock resignation of "the joy of things to come." Even Prince Charles couldn't resist joining in. "If yours is as good as this one," said Mrs Pritchard, "you'll be lucky." The visit, and the holiday, ended on that note. It had been a pleasant combination of public and private activities, and everyone – locals, holiday-makers, the Press – seemed to come away happy. As did the royal visitors, who on 23rd April arrived back at Heathrow Airport after a short flight in the

Queen's Andover, which again Prince Charles piloted home. The Prince and Princess carried out further engagements in the Duchy of Cornwall – at St Austell and the Western Woodlands – the following week.

Many people find it faintly surprising that territories as seemingly remote as the Scilly Isles should be part of the Duchy of Cornwall. To a handsome proportion of people who have never been there, they seem as distant geographically as

the Channel Islands, an impression which probably owes a lot to their connotations with long days of permanent sunshine and the subtropical characteristics of their flora. Administratively the Scillies are often thought of as being as independent and perverse as, say, the Isle of Man, but in truth there is nothing remotely unique about their status. Within only thirty miles of the Cornish Coast they are to all intents and

purposes part of Cornwall. It is therefore logical, and in any case a fact, that they also form part of the Duchy of Cornwall.

The part is only small, however – not more than three per cent. Indeed Cornwall itself contains less than a quarter of the Duchy's real estate, which is spread around Cornwall and beyond it, into Somerset, Gloucestershire and Wiltshire – and even, oddly enough, to London, where no less sacred a terrain than the Oval Cricket Ground owes its existence to the indulgence of Prince Charles as its ultimate freehold reversioner. The Oval ranks next only to Dartmoor Prison and Tintagel Castle in terms of the Duchy's celebrity properties, though unlike the Oval, Dartmoor in particular does not yield a rent. There is no lack of rent,

however, from the remainder of the Duchy's 130,000 or so acres of tenanted property. The annual figure fluctuates depending on how many properties are tenanted at any one time or, where the amount of rent depends on yields of fish or birds, according to the size of the annual harvest. But the Prince can count on a happy medium of £400,000 a year profit, of which a seemingly disproportionate chunk flows from the mere fifty acres of land leased in South London.

By a voluntary arrangement with the Government, initiated by the late Duke of Windsor in the days when Civil Lists did not provide Socialist Members of Parliament with the annual opportunity to direct broadsides against the monarchy, Prince Charles redirects a proportion of the net profit from the Duchy revenues to the Treasury. While he was a bachelor the proportion was a half. Now that he is married it is only a quarter: hence the widely circulated newspaper inaccuracy that Prince Charles had "given himself a £100,000 (or whatever) pay rise after his wedding."

Other benefits are less financially rewarding, but compensate for that in terms of quaintness. The Queen receives annual rents of single roses from time to time but Prince Charles may claim a roast leg of mutton from one

village in Dorset, any whales or porpoises washed up on the beaches of Cornwall (in the same way as the Queen Mother can, as Lord Warden of the Cinque Ports, lay claim to dead

whales found on their shores), and a whole catalogue of goods, from a pair of greyhounds to a pound of pepper, from his tenants at Launceston. In addition the Prince has the right to receive, by default as it were, the entire estate of any resident of Cornwall who dies leaving neither a will nor ascertainable next-of-kin: this is a local parallel to the operation of law in the rest of the country, whereby the goods of any person dying intestate result to the Crown as *bona vacantia* if no-one comes forward to claim as proven next-of-kin.

It is only the fact that the rank of Prince outclasses that of Duke that makes Prince Charles known more readily as Prince of Wales than as Duke of Cornwall, for the Cornish title preceded the Welsh in time. Like all Dukes of Cornwall before him, Prince Charles acquired the title automatically when his mother became Queen: it needed no documentation, no Royal Proclamation, no Parliamentary or Privy Council ratification. That was because when King Edward III created the Dukedom in 1337 in favour of his son Edward the Black Prince (the father of Richard II) the grant was made in perpetuity to the firstborn son of the reigning sovereign. It is therefore a title of

right to anyone fitting that description, though it is available to a second-born son, if the eldest son predeceases his father. The most recent example of this variation occurred when, on the accession of King Edward VII in January 1901 his second son, later King George V became Duke of Cornwall. He was the younger brother of Prince Albert Victor who had died nine years earlier at the age of twenty-eight. Not so however, to any daughter of a sovereign: thus the present Queen was never Duchess of Cornwall at any time during her father's reign, nor indeed could any female bear that title except, like the present Princess of

Wales, as the consort of a Duke of Cornwall.

By the same token it is of course possible for an heir to the throne to be Duke of Cornwall without being Prince of Wales – indeed this is always the case. The title Prince of Wales must be specifically conferred upon an heir by the sovereign and that, unlike the automatic mantle of the Duchy of Cornwall, takes time. King George V, for instance, although he became Duke of Cornwall in the instant that his grandmother Queen Victoria died and his father, Edward VII became King, became very impatient at having to wait another ten months

announcement in the Court Circular, three or four times a year, that "Today the Prince of Wales, Duke of Cornwall, toured Duchy properties in . . ." proclaims that he regards his rightful title as a source of obligation as well as of prerogative.

The Duchy of Cornwall's handsome financial surplus is not, alas, duplicated in the remainder of the Royal Family's public finances. On 10th March the Chancellor of the Exchequer announced an increase in the Queen's Civil List by an average of 8 per cent – something between the 1981 rate of inflation and the projected rate

before his father made him Prince of Wales. Remembering that frustrating delay, he conferred the same title on his own eldest son, later King Edward VIII, only a month after he himself became King.

As Duke of Cornwall, Prince Charles takes his duties as seriously as he pursued his legitimate interest in his inheritance. It was his great-great-great-grandfather, the Prince Consort, who first put the Duchy onto a sound financial footing and it has been managed faultlessly on that basis ever since. Except that occasionally

the Prince has been a little too indulgent with his tenants over rent rises, so that howls of anguish have followed the ultimate and inevitable encounters with the economic realities of life. He attends the necessary periodic meetings at Buckingham Palace, discussing financial investment, leasing, tenants' applications for development and the like. And he keeps his tenants, particularly the farming communities of the West Country and the South West peninsular, happy and loyal by his regular and frequent visits amongst them. The formal

for 1982.

Three weeks later it was disclosed that, notwithstanding the rise, the number of staff at Buckingham Palace would be reduced. In 1981, staff reductions amounted to 20 (about 6%) and a similar figure was reckoned likely this year. In addition the process would continue whereby more machinery – word-processors, switchboards, improved cooking facilities – would be installed to facilitate reductions in staff, and more work would be contracted out than before.

In the absence of definite published figures since the last financial report in 1971, the precise need and potential result of any such efforts are impossible to quantify. But as the Queen had to find over £180,000 in the last two years from her own funds to keep the books evenly balanced, it seems clear that the object is to keep that voluntary personal contribution to a minimum.

APRIL 1982

On 27th April the Duchess of Kent named a new RNLI lifeboat at the Jubilee Gardens, near County Hall, London, on the South Bank of the Thames. It was one of those occasions which in more ways than one was entirely appropriate to the Kents rather than to any other branch of the Royal Family: the ceremony took place just over three months after the Duke and Duchess had attended the Penlee lifeboat memorial service at Mousehole; the Duke of Kent is President of the RNLI as well as Grand Master of the United Grand Lodge of England; it was the Freemasons who provided the lifeboat to the Institution; and it was to be named *Duchess of Kent*.

It was the eleventh lifeboat to be given by the Freemasons in 110 years and follows a traditional link between them and the RNLI, which has resulted in almost a thousand saved lives since 1872. Constructed in glass-reinforced plastic and fitted out with the latest electronic equipment which includes echo sounders, the lifeboat can reach a speed of over 18 knots with a travelling range on a full fuel tank of almost 250 miles. The *Duchess of Kent* has joined the RNLI fleet as a relief boat peripatetically serving at stations where repairs have reduced the number of boats available.

The Duke of Atholl, Chairman of the RNLI, was present to receive the lifeboat from the Duchess on behalf of the donors, and the Duchess herself was the recipient of a small posy of flowers from Katie Higham, the daughter of the Freemasons' Grand Secretary. Katie received a present back from the Duchess, as well as a single rose from the bouquet she had just presented (left and pictures below). There followed a brief service of dedication conducted by the Rt Reverend George Reindorp, Honorary Assistant Bishop of London, after which the Duchess was invited to name the lifeboat. After an inspection on board, the Duchess, who was accompanied by her husband, watched (opposite page, right) as the lifeboat sailed off down river towards the Thames Estuary. 1982 had so far been a year of mixed fortunes for the Duchess who had celebrated, if that is the right word, her 49th birthday on 22nd February, by taking her only daughter, Lady Helen Windsor, back to Gordonstoun School for her penultimate term. Early in March, Lady Helen took ill with appendicitis and had to be rushed into a hospital at Aberdeen, where her appendix was taken out by one of the Queen's surgeons, Mr Peter Jones.

In March the Duchess, who has for some years been a regular and enthusiastic singer in the Bach Choir, had to opt out of

have made the Duchess one of the oldest ever royal mothers to be confined. The following year her gall bladder had to be removed and she was in hospital again for a brief spell. In January 1979 her mother died at the family home at Hovingham, Yorkshire, and two months later the Duchess went into hospital suffering from mental strain.

The long spell of recuperation seemed to do the trick, but in 1981 she slipped a disc in her neck and had to wear a collar. After the latest operation, the Duchess was out of hospital within a few days and able to resume her official engagements – appropriately enough, the opening of a surgery at Burnham Market in Norfolk on 7th April.

On 21st April the Duchess again saw her daughter off to Gordonstoun – this time in the company of Prince Edward, as both cousins were about to begin their final term there. Like Prince Edward, Lady Helen Windsor was one of the clutch of royal babies born within two months of each other in 1964.

the Choir's trip to Hong Kong at Easter because of the possibility that she and the Duke would also be paying an official visit there. This disappointment proved a blessing in disguise, because as Easter approached the Duchess was taken into King Edward VII Hospital for Officers in Marylebone – just a month after her sister-in-law Princess Michael had left – to undergo an operation for a similar complaint, the removal of a "benign obstruction" from the gall bladder duct.

The operation, performed by another of the Queen's physicians Sir John Batten, was short and successful, but her spell in hospital brought to mind the catalogue of indispositions suffered by the Duchess in the previous five years. In October 1977 she miscarried her fourth baby, a late potential addition to the family whose birth would

She was the third of them, born on April 28th and the three imaginative portraits of her (overleaf) by Lord Snowdon, released to celebrate her 18th birthday, make you wonder what happened to the years in between. "Keeping out of the limelight" – a favourite journalistic phrase for reticent royalty – seems to be a full-time job for parents in the junior branches of the Royal Family, and the Duke and Duchess of Kent, whose second child Lady Helen is, have done that job very efficiently. Apart from the occasional official portraits of her – only the ones taken by her father when she was fourteen came near to the classic pose Lord Snowdon has caught – she has featured only at grand royal occasions such as the Silver Jubilee, the Queen Mother's 80th birthday celebrations and last year's Royal Wedding. Just now and again she has been

photographed on the ski slopes of the French Alps, or on the way to school at Gordonstoun, which she and Prince Edward left in July. Her final term at co-educational Gordonstoun – its complement includes 70 girls – ended with her taking 'A' levels in English, Art and the History of Art and she seems set for a course at art school if she is successful. Unfortunately she was at school when her eighteenth birthday came round but her parents had already thrown a party for her at Anmer, their house on the Sandringham estate, a couple of weeks beforehand, during the Easter holidays.

At the time of his birth in

he has been able to choose his own career and in doing so has followed unarguably artistic inclinations. By temperament he is nothing like the bohemian envisaged by the early newspaper article, but his motley combination of clothes – black suede shoes, striped jacket, vivid cerise shirt, jeans supported by a pink and blue "Charles Loves Diana" belt – proclaim an antipathy for respectable stereotypes. Now on the verge of his 21st birthday he is branching out into life with an independence which no member of the Royal Family has had the opportunity to enjoy since Lord Harewood in the early 1950's.

November 1961, Viscount Linley's future attracted more than the usual amount of speculation. One Fleet Street columnist imagined him at the age of 20 swanning around the Latin Quarter of Paris, frequenting café terraces and the haunts of the artists of the Left Bank. It was not a bad guess: strictly speaking a non-royal member of the Queen's family,

Two years ago he left Bedales School – where his sister Lady Sarah Armstrong-Jones was also a pupil – with 'O' and 'A' Levels in Design, after a school career which had been spent pursuing his vocational subjects – art, pottery, painting – as fully as the general curriculum allowed. He enrolled at the John Makepeace School of Woodcraft at Parnham House – a beautiful Elizabethan

disciplines of office management and marketing.

Viscount Linley's own forte is in design work, but when it comes to the working of wood he is no slouch. He has a predeliction for light, "fun," modern furniture and for the subtle colour and textural effects which dyes and stains provide. His favourite wood is sycamore, with its "clean, fresh, challenging look," and two of his first four commercial products, a low table and a screen, evidence his fondness for it.

In July he graduated from the School, but not before he had started work on the next stage of his career – arranging with a fellow graduate, Charles

mansion set deep in lush, wooded Dorset countryside not far from Beaminster, where these pictures were taken in June 1982.

"It was Bedales who gave me the incentive to come here," he explains, and he has never regretted his decision.

"Parnham's not the sort of place where you have doubts," is probably his best compliment to his *alma mater,* where, almost claustrophobically distant from the high life, students work away willingly throughout the day and well into the night. "We're quite happy to stay in," he says: "there are lights on in the workshops almost every night."

The School's guiding principle is a simple one – a preparation for independence. Students are taught not merely how to make things out of wood: they are instructed in the skills of drawing and drafting, appraisal of the quality and characteristics of wood, and the ancillary

Wheeler-Carmichael, and two previous graduates from the school, to take the lease of a workshop in Dorking where he puts the School's precepts into action by producing and marketing furniture, hand made to his own design. He is in the enviable position of being able to accept only those commissions he knows he will enjoy carrying out, and only a small proportion of his work will involve mass production – and that on a very limited scale. Some of his work has found sufficient favour with his mother, Princess Margaret, to be installed at Kensington Palace, and Lord Snowdon, who paid several visits to his son at Parnham House, has frequently expressed a degree of satisfaction at his success for everyone to know how rewarding all his encouragement has been to him.

APRIL 1982

Prince Charles spent a full twelve-hour schedule in Wales on 30th April when he carried out four major engagements in Carmarthen and Cardiff.
The main purpose of his visit to Carmarthen was to receive the Freedom of the town on behalf of the Welsh Guards, of which he is Colonel. The arrangements for the visit had caused an embarrassing dispute when the Mayor of Carmarthen, Mr Peter Griffiths, declared that he was a pacifist and while he had nothing against Prince Charles personally, he did not want to meet him or bestow any honours

Colonel's uniform he arrived from Carmarthen's County Hall in an open landau, at Carmarthen Park (below and bottom) where the freedom ceremony was due to take place. Accompanied by the new Mayor, the Prince inspected the parade (top picture) before they all made their way (centre picture and opposite page bottom left) to the dais in the middle of the Park. In accepting the Freedom on behalf of his Regiment, Prince Charles explained (opposite page, top centre) that three hundred troops had been taken off exercises in the Brecon

upon him in his capacity as Colonel of an armed regiment. The town Council applied to the Regiment to ask if the engagement could be put back until August, when the new Mayor was due to be appointed, but the probability of a posting abroad made it impossible for the Regiment to agree.
Accordingly the Council decided to bring forward the mayor-making ceremony to 28th April, two days before the Prince's visit. The creation of a new mayor also involved the appointment of a new sheriff, and the outgoing sheriff, 70-year-old Mr Evan Lewis, resigned in protest.
By the time Prince Charles arrived, some two months later, these difficulties had been conveniently forgotten and, wearing his impressive full dress

Beacons for the day: "Their arduous training in the Welsh hills is designed to prepare them for possible deployment in the South Atlantic," he said.
After taking the Salute (far right) as the Guards marched past with bayonets fixed, he left the Park, and changed into undress

uniform for a walkabout from Shire Hall to St Peter's Civic Hall. He met the occasional old campaigner (opposite page, bottom left) and received the usual plethora of small bouquets from the local townspeople

(above). Once inside the Civic Hall he signed the Roll of Town Freemen and received a memento of the occasion in the form of a silver Welsh Dragon (overleaf, right hand page). Prince Charles took lunch privately and, having changed once again into civvies, left for Cambria School, where he opened new extensions, unveiled a commemorative plaque, and spoke to some of the school's pupils (overleaf). Half an hour later he was on his way to Carmarthen's new leisure centre, which he formally

APRIL 1982

in 1545 and that in consequence either of uncannily accurate French gunfire or appallingly inadequate navigation, she keeled over, and hit the sea bed ten fathoms down at an angle of 60°, just a mile from shore, off Southsea.

King Henry VIII, whose pride and joy the Mary Rose was, was standing on the tower of Southsea Castle watching her progress when the disaster happened, and was not amused. No attempt was made to salvage her – a hopeless task at the time – and she lay there until she was discovered by Alexander

opened, and where he visited the gymnasium, fencing club and mother-and-toddler group (opposite page, top left). After a quick tea at the Centre the Prince left for Cardiff's City Hall, where he attended a banquet given by the Asian Society in Wales, and watched a display of classical Indian dancing. His day finished at 10.30 pm –12½ hours after the official start. Fortunately it was a Friday, and the beginning of a long May Day Bank Holiday weekend.

Two days earlier, Prince Charles had clambered aboard the barge (opposite page centre right) belonging to the Mary Rose Trust to prepare for the ninth dive he has undertaken to view the latest progress in raising the now celebrated flagship which sank 437 years ago. No-one knows quite why she went down: the record shows only that she left Portsmouth one day

McKee, the historian and diver, after he had spotted her possible whereabouts on an old naval chart.

The operation to raise her was conceived almost twenty years ago, and preliminary explorations began in 1965. In the last two years a whole museum of objects has been removed from within the ship; the vast majority of which have been incredibly well preserved by the silt which has gently cocooned the hull for four centuries. In fact the range of armaments, supplies, clothing, tools and instruments has long distinguished the wreck as a unique time capsule. Excavators have discovered and recovered everything from cannons to musical instruments, long-bows to surgical equipment, the bones of dogs to sandals complete with straw padding intact. Over a hundred bodies, out of the 700 lost, have been brought up in

inspect a newly-excavated hole in her stern – for forty minutes. He once remarked jocularly that the water is usually like lentil soup, but visibility today was comparatively good at three to four yards. Closed circuit TV monitored him as he obtained his first clear view of the shape of the hull and its superstructure. "The timbers are in marvellous condition," he said afterwards. "I could see the deck and the gun ports."

The project, whose aim is to have the remains of the wreck displayed as the centre-piece of a naval history museum in Portsmouth, is costing upwards of £4 million, of which £1½ million still needs to be found. Recent contributions include the latest instalment of a £350,000

gift from the National Heritage Memorial Fund, offered on a pound-for-pound basis, £200,000 claimable from the Government following the wreck's designation as a national monument in February, and the Ministry of Defence's promise of a team of Royal Engineers to help lift her as part of a training exercise for divers.

such a state of preservation that it has been possible to discern archers from seamen by reference to their comparative muscle development. The archaeological director, Margaret Rule, even hopes that the body of the ship's Admiral, Sir George Carew, will be retrieved, complete with chain of office, with the bosun's whistle attached, which Henry VIII presented to him the day before the ship set sail.

The Prince of Wales, as President of the Mary Rose Trust, unashamedly admits the "overdeveloped sense of history" which prompts his unceasing interest in the project. He finds it "fascinating to dive amongst the wreckage." On one dive he was exploring one part of the hull which had been broken into and came face to face with "a great grinning skull – it had marvellous teeth! It was like something out of Jaws." On another he tried to use the suction hose designed to take away quantities of unwanted mud and silt, but he found it laid claim much more readily to his trowel and even his arm! And he was fascinated by the number of lobsters that have already found their way into the ship's remains and are steadily tucking into her and her contents.

His final dive before the raising operation begins in October was no disappointment. Well padded against the icy waters of the Solent by his orange and black dry-suit (right), he swam in sixty feet of water – fifteen feet deeper than the ship, so that he could

MAY 1982

tour of St John's Market, the opening of the new headquarters of the Merseyside Police, a concert given by the Royal Liverpool Philharmonic Orchestra and a visit to Liverpool Town Hall. Merseysiders are not known for their unrestrained enthusiasm for the monarchy and there was the almost inevitable sour note as the Queen and the Duke of Edinburgh approached the Town Hall. A group of about thirty protesters began to wave banners calling for "Reality not Royalty" and chanting slogans. There were scuffles as other sections of the two thousand strong crowd began to tear down

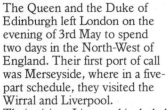

The Queen and the Duke of Edinburgh left London on the evening of 3rd May to spend two days in the North-West of England. Their first port of call was Merseyside, where in a five-part schedule, they visited the Wirral and Liverpool.
Their visit to Liverpool included these happy scenes during their

Stephenson, a patient since he swallowed camphorated oil a few days before, forgot his lines of welcome and threw a tantrum in front of the Queen. He threw his Union Jack at her, missing her by inches when she darted smartly to one side, spilled his set of bricks over the floor in

the banners and sing the National Anthem. Five people were arrested in the fracas which the Queen, with her usual practised calm, appeared not to notice.

In the Wirral they toured the new £29 million Arrowe Park Hospital, an engagement which provided its own brand of light relief when young Lewis

front of her, stuck a plastic bucket over his head and refused to speak to her. Fortunately for him and for his red-faced mother, the Queen was enormously amused.

There was more amusement next day when she and Prince Philip toured Granada Television's new *Coronation Street* set during their visit to Greater Manchester. They met almost the whole cast, including Peter Adamson and Barbara Knox (top left) – alias Len and Rita Fairclough; Bernard Youens and Jean Alexander (bottom

"That would take rather a long time," the Queen said to him. Len Fairclough introduced a rare note of gravity when he assured the Queen of the cast's concern for Prince Andrew's safety in the South Atlantic. "It must be a

very worrying time for you and your family," he said. "Our hearts are with you."
Another of the original cast of the programme, which has been running for twenty-one years, was Doris Speed (Annie Walker)

left) as Stan and Hilda Ogden; and Alf Roberts, owner of the Street's corner shop.
The repartee flew in all directions, mainly at Prince Philip's instance. He asked Julie Goodyear (Bet Lynch) whether the Rover's Return was open yet. She flashed a smile and her enormous Charles-and-Diana disc earrings at him and said, "Not at the moment, but I'd pull a pint for you any time." The Prince roared with laughter when Patricia Phoenix (Elsie Tanner) said, "I'm one of the original cast. But I'm decaying with the Street. I'm in need of

renovation." She was also introduced to the Queen. "Meet the Queen of Coronation Street," said the Chairman of Granada to the Queen. "Meet the Queen," said the Queen to Miss Phoenix. Hilda Ogden, reluctantly and only on instructions from above, took out her legendary curlers for the occasion. Her "husband" asked the Queen if he could have a contract to clean Buckingham Palace's windows.

who was told years ago, when she went to Buckingham Palace to receive her MBE, that the Queen was a regular watcher of *Coronation Street*. The Queen Mother is rumoured to be another royal enthusiast.
The royal visit to the new £170,000 set lasted for almost half an hour, and was only one of several engagements in Manchester that day. The Queen and Prince Philip had earlier inspected exhibits at the new Museum of Science and Industry, where they saw displays illustrating examples of restoration and renewal projects within the Greater Manchester area. They also met young people employed on Manpower Services Commission schemes run in tandem with the local Council, and viewed the Council's large collection of civic plate and historical memorabilia at the Town Hall. Here they

signed the Distinguished Visitors' Book (opposite, top right), before going out into Albert Square for a ten-minute walk to Princess Street.

The brief 100-yard walkabout provided the local people with one of their best opportunities to get close to the Queen. As always, those with the most colourful accoutrements, whether flags, banners, balloons or Union Jack umbrellas, attracted the royal eye, but the Queen and Prince Philip also found time to exchange a few well chosen remarks with lines of smartly-dressed school girls

(bottom left) and colourfully dressed representatives of Manchester's ethnic communities (opposite page bottom right), and to accept an attractive posy of flowers from a chairbound pensioner (below left) who could probably have regaled the Queen with a host of reminiscences about royal visits to Manchester.

A visit to Manchester University followed. The Queen opened the John Rylands Library and received a portfolio of old photographs and a specially bound book about the University, while the Duke

listened to part of a discussion about the cotton trade, before the royal party had lunch. The Manchester visit ended with a tour of Withington Hospital to meet staff and students and to look at displays on aerodynamics, a fairly lofty subject on which to end the royal couple's two-day visit in the north-west.

MAY 1982

In the age of growing generation gaps, a culture gap yawned between royalty and a rock group when Prince Charles arrived (below) to attend a concert given by the heavy metal rock band Status Quo at Birmingham's National Exhibition Centre on 14th May. Even the Prince, who met the group (right) after the concert, told them he wished he had worn jeans, and the group agreed that it would have been a turn-on if he had. "Everyone would have freaked out," said the lead singer Francis Rossi. They thoughtfully provided ear plugs for him, though he equally thoughtfully declined to use them, and he was relieved to know that they didn't encourage their fans to indulge in head-banging. And they were worried on his behalf about his behaviour at the concert. "Anyone who sits down at a Quo concert gets lynched," said rhythm guitarist Rick Parfitt.

"And I don't think he knows." In the end it all went well enough. The audience, 11,000-strong in denims and sweatshirts, applauded the Prince longer than anyone in the Festival Hall does, and he applauded the group at all the right moments. The Prince's Trust, for whose benefit the evening was staged, came off £70,000 to the good and Rick Parfitt ("I've always been a great Royalist") was thrilled to be shaking the Prince's hand afterwards. "By all accounts he's a bit of a raver," he said. "Well, after all," said bass guitarist Alan Lancaster, "he is the same age as we are. He grew up in the rock era."
So he did. And it's worth

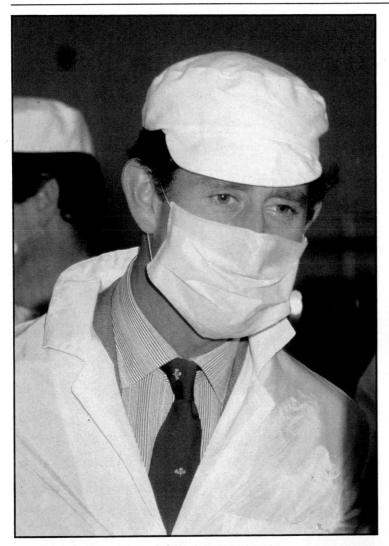

remembering that Status Quo have been around almost as long. They claimed this United Kingdom tour as their twentieth anniversary tour, thus treating their second year at Sedgehill Comprehensive School in Beckenham as their inaugural year. Most of the group were then thirteen. And through all the heavy metal image comes a hint of respectable gratification: "It's a unique achievement in British rock . . . fully deserved for a band who've slogged it right through from their schooldays. Theirs is a story of hard work and perseverance, sometimes when it seemed that the odds against them were just

too high; yet they've always made it through, never losing sight of the fans that made their success possible."

Prince Charles was back on quieter duties – and in Wales again – when he visited Control Data, the high technology plant at Brynmawr on 3rd June, and is seen (above & above left) in part of the "White Room," a 60,000 square feet clean area designed to preserve the sensitivity of coating material to be applied to the plant's tape and memory disc products. The factory was established in 1965 and has the capacity to produce double the nation's present demand for computer tape and discs.

Earlier that day the Prince had visited the British Steel Corporation Workshop for Small Businesses at Port Talbot (left), where he spoke with employees as they made a whole range of ornamental models (opposite page, bottom pictures), and toured Nantyglo Comprehensive School near Brynmawr.

The Badminton Horse Trials have their parallel in the Horse Show world in terms of permanence, excellence and royal patronage.

That well-established five day domestic equestrian event, the Royal Windsor Horse Show, took place from 12th to 16th May and as always the Royal Family was represented, though, as at Badminton, in a purely private capacity. The Queen, who had missed Badminton because of the hastily-arranged visit to Ottawa to sign over the Canadian Constitution, did not,

in spite of the looming conflict in the South Atlantic, have to forego her usual attendance at Home Park Windsor.

The Show, which is held totally out of doors, brings together the varying skills of show-jumping, carriage driving, Pony Club games and dressage displays, as well as the spectacular military-style entertainments by the King's Troop Royal Horse Artillery and the Household

Cavalry. This particular year the main interest in the show-jumping arena was drawn by the intense competition the British riders faced from several foreign entrants – the Australians, Belgians, Swedes and Libyans, all going for a total of £12,000 in prize money.

The Queen's presence on 14th, 15th and 16th May matched the days on which the International Carriage Driving Grand Prix, sponsored as usual by the London firm of estate agents, Messrs. Knight Frank & Rutley,

was held. This was no coincidence since, again as usual, the Duke of Edinburgh took part in that competition, in this, the tenth year of his career in competitive carriage driving in the international field.

The first day's competition centred around dressage, which covers a multitude of fine and well-scrutinised points of performance and style, such as the forward and backwards manoeuvring of the teams of horses while hitched to the carriages, the condition and presentation of both horses and carriages, and the dress, deportment and behaviour of the drivers themselves. Prince Philip (right and opposite page, top right) was as immaculate as ever with his black topper showing a perfect sheen, white cravat, brown leather gloves and regulation apron, his superbly turned-out metal-framed carriage and his equally well-groomed horses fresh from the Royal Mews.

Competition was keen, however, with George Bowman, seven times winner of the British National Championships,

heading no fewer than thirteen British competitors, and five further entrants from Europe and the United States. No wonder the Prince looked concerned, and the Queen thoughtful, as (left and opposite page far left) they watched and discussed the progress of the other riders. (With them, incidentally, was Prince Philip's youngest, and only surviving sister, 68-year-old Princess

Sophie of Hanover, a regular visitor to the Royal Windsor Horse Show.)
The Queen, surrounded by tournament officials and by members of her staff, including (below right) the Crown Equerry, Lt-Col Sir John Miller, himself an accomplished four-in-

illustrious twenty-five year polo-playing career. His choice of what was then a relatively little-known sport betrayed his typical, almost perverse flair for trying anything once, and he was undeterred by its comparatively novel and unrecognised status. Indeed, the year before had seen

learn all there is to learn about dealing with horses in any context.
He probably realised this when, after feeling understandably pleased with himself at the end of his first season, the following one brought him down to earth with a catalogue of disasters

large and small. The most spectacular was the famous accident at the Lowther Driving Trials, the well-established annual event at Shap, on the edge of the Lake District, in 1972, when the rear of his carriage hit a tree stump, and horses, passengers – royal and

hand driver, was seen at her most relaxed, interested and animated as she followed the fortunes of her husband's many rivals round the dressage course. Both Prince Philip and his team of horses performed well, and their end-of-day positions gave them a unique opportunity to carry off first prize by the end of the tournament.
Four-in-hand carriage driving is now Prince Philip's most consuming competitive sport. He took it up in 1971, as he charismatically says, "because I thought it was the right thing to do," though his decision was more than probably prompted by the mild arthritis in his hands which effectively drew the curtain on his enthusiastic and

only the first internationally recognised carriage-driving event, so the sport could hardly be said to be very advanced in respectability.
His apprenticeship, much of it self-taught, lasted a couple of hard-working years. He began by mastering the art of guiding single horses drawing carriages, graduated to pairs of horses and finally, with the aid of miniature training courses which he ordered to be laid out at Windsor and Sandringham, cracked the secret of coping with four horses at a time. Perhaps "cracking the secret" sounds too final: it is in fact inaccurate, and the Duke is nothing if not disarmingly realistic, knowing full well that you never quite

commoner – and conveyance were thrown all over the place. It was after that, when the righted carriage was found to be badly knocked about and not fit for further use without considerable expenditure on repairs, that he went in for metal-framed rather than wooden-framed vehicles. "I knew I was asking for all sorts of new trouble when I took it up," he once said, and his career from that point has proved his foresight. To the common herd, leaders and wheelers and swingletrees are so much equestrian jargon, and carriage driving is news only when carriages are upturned, wheels are stuck in mud, shoulders are dislocated, language turns blue, and drivers become thoroughly soaked in lakes and streams. In his time Prince Philip has been associated with all of these fond and, to those not directly involved, somewhat amusing visions, but he takes the knocks philosophically: "Anyone who is concerned about his dignity would be well advised to keep away from horses," he once wrote. "Horses are great levellers. I've got shoulders which would make interesting specimens for any medical school."

For all that, his eleven years in charge of the reins have

produced some satisfying results. He has won prizes at competitions all over Great Britain, from Scotland to Cirencester, from Cheshire to Goodwood. In 1975, having come seventh in the Royal Scottish Championships, fifth at Cirencester and a creditable fourth at Windsor, he was

selected for the European Driving Championships in Poland, just two years after he first competed internationally. In 1980 he captained the British team in the World Championships and it came back victorious. Last year he was fifth at the Windsor Horse Trials, though unplaced in the

enjoy in London.

The Queen has about three dozen ceremonial horses at the Royal Mews at any one time. The dozen or so greys are known as Windsor Greys (simply because their predecessors were kept at the Windsor stables until they were closed down just before the

importance until recently, is beginning to take over.

Prince Philip prefers the slightly nippier characteristics of part-bred Cleveland Bays and it was these he used at the Royal Windsor Horse Show this year. They stood him in good stead in the cross-country event, or Marathon, on 15th May, when

his own supple and authoritative horsemanship and the fitness of his team brought him through a near faultless round – even though his passengers may on occasion have experienced that frisson of fear which turns the knuckles white (below left). But the Queen looked pleased

European Championships in Switzerland. In all he has come second four times at Windsor. He was hoping to improve on that in 1982.

Much of his success must of course depend on his horses and he has the good fortune to be able to pick from the Royal Mews stock for each occasion. This is not so outrageous as it might at first glance seem, since

the purpose to which the Queen's pageant horses are put is by and large that of pulling carriages. Granted, the events for which they are officially used are ceremonial, but this does not make them unsuitable for competitive carriage driving, and the occasional testing on a gruelling Horse Show course provides them with better exercise than they can ever

Second World War), or as Oldenburg Greys. The latter strain now predominates, and indeed were used to haul the Prince and Princess of Wales' 1902 State Postillion carriage from St Paul's Cathedral on their Wedding Day. Then there are two dozen bay horses, well represented by Oldenburgs, though the Cleveland strain, which has enjoyed secondary

enough with his performance (opposite page), while his youngest son Prince Edward (top), on weekend leave from Gordonstoun, was quietly impressed. It was hard to believe that his father was on the verge of his sixty-first birthday.

Next day, the obstacle course brought the competition to its end. The Queen, rather more formally dressed in a light suit –

a concession to the fact that she would later take part in the official formalities and prize-giving, sat in the stands with her sister-in-law (below and opposite page) recording the thrills and spills of the event with her ever-present camera. Prince Philip, back in formal dress again after the cloth cap and short sleeves of the day before, turned in another good performance and a clear round, and to his great delight, carried off first prize for the first time. His reward was a rosette from the Queen, to whom he respectfully doffed his topper (left) and a place in the

British team for the World Championships in the Netherlands in August. Prince Philip has rarely missed an opportunity to write or contribute to books on subjects close to his heart. He has in his time written articles or forewords on yachting, painting, birds, the environment, flora and fauna and architecture. Last year he began work on an authoritative book on competitive carriage driving. His victory at the Royal Windsor – "the most satisfying win of my driving career" – should give the book all the authority it needs. Any budding four-in-hand enthusiast should consider taking a leaf or two out of it.

MAY 1982

The season of that other absorbing sporting pursuit of the Royal Family, polo, began in mid-May, and the royal goings-on at the Royal Windsor Horse Show were rivalled by equally enthusiastic participation on the polo fields of Brockenhurst, Ham and Windsor that weekend by none other than the Prince of Wales.

Prince Charles, it is almost staggering to record, has been playing polo for eighteen years – over half of his still relatively young life. His earliest tuition began while he was still a schoolboy at Gordonstoun: Prince Philip, keen to provide him with the opportunity of

Tournament between two local teams, Foresters and New Park, in aid of the Mountbatten Memorial Fund. Prince Charles arrived from Broadlands, where he and his wife were staying for the weekend with Lord and Lady Romsey, to a crowd of only five hundred people – an unusually low gate for a royal polo match but probably explained by the lack of publicity which attended his arrival.

The Princess of Wales arrived a little later with the Romseys and spent some time watching the game: Prince Charles scored a goal for Foresters but they still lost the match. For much of the

boiling hot afternoon the Princess was entertained by the attentions of small children. She was sitting at a table, sipping, it is said, a glass of cold rum punch, when four-year-old Alice Kennard pushed her way towards her and said "Would you like to see my baby?" It happened that the baby was Alice's doll, Polly. The Princess picked Polly up for several minutes and said, "I think your baby's very nice. I hope mine will be as good."

A little later two small girls – one of which was the daughter of one of Prince Charles' team-mates for the day – stood against the cordon near the Princess, in

enjoying a sport he himself revelled in and at which he excelled, gave his son lessons during school holidays. A well-known series of press photographs exists showing the young Prince looking not entirely attentive or convinced as his father demonstrates various points of polo technique.

But it seems Prince Charles was giving all the attention he needed to. At Cambridge University, he won his half-blue and he continued to play so regularly that his handicap improved rapidly, in spite of his Service career which took him abroad for long periods of time. Since he left the Services he has been heavily committed to playing polo on every available weekend throughout the four-month season, and since 1979 has played so competitively that he has been engaged to play in some of the very best teams.

The match he took part in at Brockenhurst on 15th May was the Mountbatten Memorial Day

French horse-racing family. Coincidentally for the royal prospective father, Geoffrey van Hay, a polo-playing friend of the Prince's who happened to be there, heard that his own wife had just given birth to their baby. "Perhaps you should have been there for the birth," the Prince told him.

Meanwhile the Princess of Wales had taken delivery, at Broadlands, of a new dark blue 1.6 litre Ford Escort Ghia, which had been ordered for her to replace her old Ford Escort. After a few trial runs round the estate in her new acquisition, she drove herself home to Highgrove House where Prince

silent admiration of her. The Princess got up, ducked under the rope, and had a brief conversation with them, before resuming her place to finish off a plate of strawberries and cream. Both the Princess and, later, the Prince returned to Broadlands for the night. Next afternoon Prince Charles was off again, to play polo at Ham, near Richmond (left). This time his arrival was enthusiastically greeted by a capacity ground as his blue Aston Martin showed up (top left). A quick change (centre pictures) and he was ready to captain Windsor Great Park against Ham, captained by Guy Wildenstein, of the wealthy

Charles joined her later that evening.

He, meanwhile, had left Ham for Windsor, where, at the Guards' Polo club, he was to play (opposite page, top pictures) for the Towry Law Cup. He could not have wished for a better start to the season: his team won and (overleaf) Prince Charles celebrated in the usual way by drinking champagne from the trophy. The 1982 polo season, which ended in September, was one of the casualties of the conflict over the Falkland Islands and the consequently severed relations with Argentina. In the same way that Tottenham Hospur tactfully

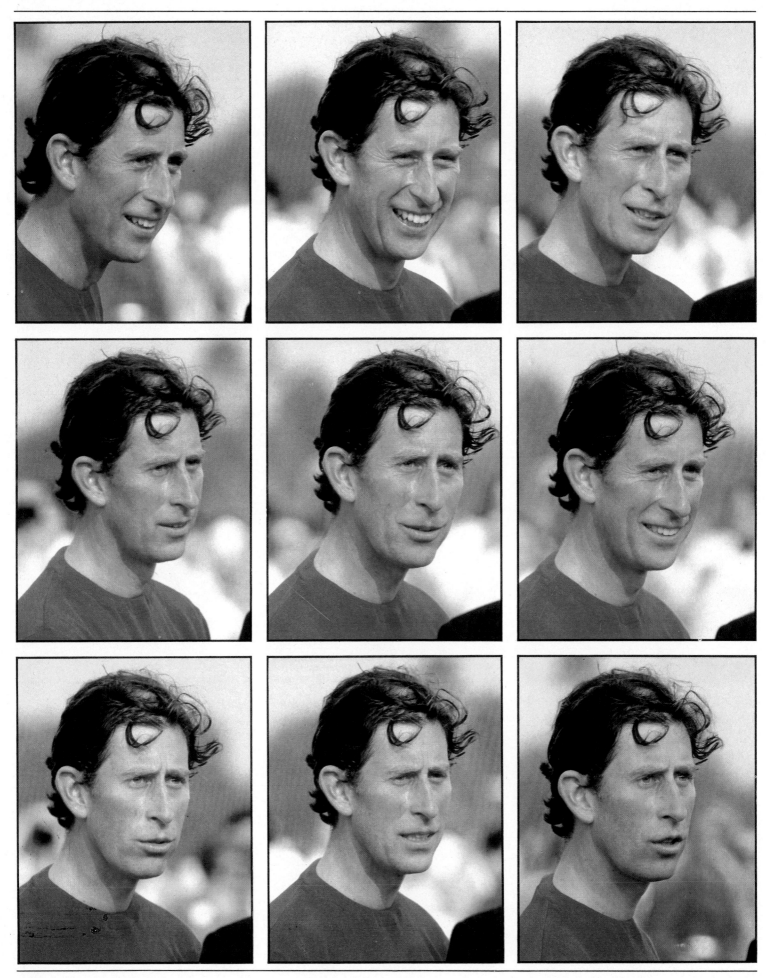

withdrew their only available Argentinian player, Villa, from the FA Cup Final in May, so the major polo clubs in England suspended the usual practice of importing Argentinian players into their teams for the season's games. Simultaneously, the trade in polo ponies, habitually brought across from Argentina with their players and breeders at the start of the season, was halted by the economic sanctions being applied against the Argentinians. The result was that a large number of British players took part in major polo tournaments this year, and that the quality of ponies was not up to the usual standard.

Prince Charles who, like his father, enjoys several connections with Argentinian

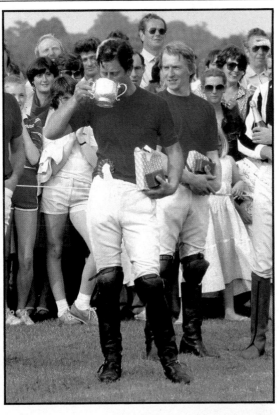

polo players and enthusiasts, was not entirely unaffected by the consequences of the Falklands dispute. In mid-April a potentially embarrassing situation was anticipated when it was learned that he had recently hired an Argentinian called Raoul Correa to act as stable groom to his string of polo ponies, with responsibility for ensuring that they were brought to peak condition for each successive match. This appointment, to fill the gap left by another Argentinian, Rafael Pinero, whom Prince Charles had engaged on loan in 1981, was made before the Falklands crisis began, so that there could be no criticism of the Prince for having made the choice. And, although a few die-hards thought it bad form for him to be riding polo ponies groomed by "one of the enemy," the discovery that Correa was in fact a naturalised Briton, holding a British

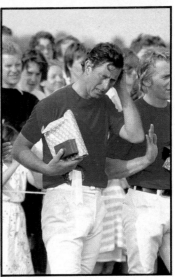

passport, married to a British-born wife, and had lived in Britain for the last thirteen years, seemed to despatch the anticipated crisis almost as soon as it had surfaced.

Nevertheless, the game as a whole suffered the loss of the two most prestigious Anglo-Argentinian tournaments of the season – the Ambassadors Cup matches at Windsor and Cowdray Park Sussex, where last year, as in previous years, a large contingent of the Royal Family joined Argentinian diplomats to watch a series of excellent, hard-fought matches.

MAY 1982

Queen Mother, but the previous month it was announced that she would not be available, and the engagement was hastily tacked on to the Princess of Wales' schedule. As it happened it was an apt enough alternative. The Princess had early in February assumed the presidency of five organisations, four of them orientated towards benefiting young people, and one of them was the Albany Trust.

The Albany Trust is one of those little-known, very localised charities which achieve any degree of celebrity only on an occasion such as this. In fact it has long been associated with

Prompted in no small measure by a spell of warm weather, a colourful carnival atmosphere permeated the South East London suburb of Deptford when on 18th May the Princess of Wales performed the last of her official engagements before the birth of Prince William. She was there to open a new community centre, erected at a cost of almost £3 million through the good offices of the Albany Trust. The opening was to have been performed by the

the Royal Family – indeed it began under the auspices of none other than H.R.H. the Duchess of Albany. She was the wife of Queen Victoria's youngest, and only haemophiliac, son Prince Leopold (1853-1884), who in

1881 was created Duke of Albany. A homely, good-natured woman, she devoted her life to good causes, particularly after the death of her husband, to whom she had been married for less than three years.
One cause she espoused with

Eventually the exploitation was halted, but the Duchess and the Minister found that they had, well-meaningly but unwittingly, created their own little unemployment problem. With the prospect of seeing the girls on the streets making their own dubious efforts to employ themselves gainfully, the Duchess decided to put right the mischief she had created, and in 1894 established a Trust, which has borne her name ever since, designed to cater for the girls in their long hours of enforced idleness.

When the Duchess, whose sister Queen Emma was the great-

her inimitable brand of crusading zeal was against the exploitation of adolescent girls in the Deptford area, who at a time of considerable poverty and squalor were being employed in slaughter-houses and in the rag trade for scandalously low rates of pay. The Duchess spent much of her time trying to locate the Whitehall official who might be able to put a stop to the practice, and finally found a Minister whom she knew well enough to persuade to take up the cudgels on her behalf.

grandmother of the present Queen Beatrix of the Netherlands, died in 1922, her only daughter, the late Princess Alice, Countess of Athlone, took over the presidency, which she held until her own death fifty-nine years later at the age of 97. That was in January 1981. Two years earlier she had button-holed her great-great-nephew Prince Charles and persuaded him to lay the foundation stone of the Community Centre which his wife was now in Deptford to open formally (these pages).

The Princess of Wales spent over an hour at the centre, receiving the usual heaps of posies from the crowds she spoke to during the visit, and looking at her most contented. She did not, however, forgo any opportunity to sit down nor, as one might have come by now to expect, to talk about babies. With her own confinement

expected only six weeks later, the creche was the focus of great interest. She also met those who give their time voluntarily to help in the centre, watched a group of pensioners at a bingo session and visited the centre's restaurant – and it was here that mothers and children heard of the latest preparations for the royal birth.

The stories didn't quite tally and no-one was quite sure whether the Princess said that her baby *would* be a boy or that she hoped it would. "We'll just have to wait and see," she finally told 14-year-old David Rowland. She took one look at Mrs Patricia Woodgates' five-month-old twins and confessed "I don't think I could cope with a brace. I only hope I can cope with one

when the time comes." Mrs Woodgates warned her that "you don't learn much about them until you've actually had them," a remark that put into perspective the Princess' revelation to Mrs Doreen Markland, that Prince Charles had been studying books about pregnancy and baby care so feverishly of late that he had become "something of an expert. He keeps telling me what to do," she added, "and I don't like it!"

The visit came to an end with

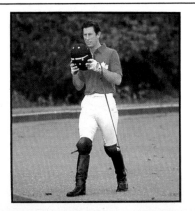

the presentation to the Princess of a picture of the community centre drawn by Mr Reg Rowlands, the Chairman of the New Cross Building Society. The old Duchess of Albany would have been proud of her achievement.

With official engagements over until October (as it was then thought) the Princess was expected to remain out of public sight for the foreseeable future. The precedent which had always

(these pages) in which he played for the Canadian side run by the biscuit heir Mr Galen Weston. It wasn't, however, the best of days: the wind was chilly and she ventured only short distances from the car, where she frequently sheltered, looking just a little bored.

kept royal ladies discreetly indoors during the visible stages of their pregnancies had already been broken and many people expected that time would now be called. But the Princess of Wales has not been called innovatory for nothing and she turned up in public almost as often as there was a polo match to see in which Prince Charles was playing. Giving the lie to the widely believed story, created out of her reactions to some pretty terrifying scenes on the field in 1981, that she disliked polo, she followed Prince Charles almost everywhere, pacing the perimeters with the informality for which she has become well known.

Thus on 22nd May she travelled with the Prince to Windsor Great Park for a weekend game

MAY 1982

They change the Guard here, ambassadors are officially accredited here, an obscure Epiphany service is held in its chapel once a year, and in the old days Royal Levées were held here in what was then called "the Season."
One could be readily forgiven for supposing that, as far as official or public appearances are concerned, the Royal Family seems to take a dim view of St James's, and give it a wide berth.

St James's Palace is one of the more obscure of London's royal buildings. Not physically, for its long, Georgian-windowed walls can be skirted at any time of day by anyone wishing to get from Trafalgar Square to Piccadilly by road. But for all the security surrounding it, Buckingham Palace is known far more intimately than St James's. As the diplomatic focal point of the royal connection, St James's wears a reputation even more forbidding than its dark frontage.

Visits by its members are conspicuous by their rarity. The occasional concert, exhibition or fashion show is staged here from time to time, and may draw a royal audience or patron. This was where the Prince and Princess of Wales exhibited their wedding presents during two hectic and profitable months in 1981, and where Prince and Princess Michael of Kent have had their two children christened. Like every State Visitor to this country before

him, the Sultan of Oman came here to receive addresses of welcome during his State Visit in March this year.
Both the Duke of Kent and his sister Princess Alexandra have their London offices here, and for the Kents, York House at the western end of the Palace is their official London residence.
So the Duchess of Kent did not have very far to come when on the morning of 24th May she made a very special presentation to fifty handicapped children.

Yard was spectacularly exciting. Each coach was festooned with balloons and streamers and would shortly take them all on a tour of London before their journeys back to their home towns.

The Duchess found the occasion both moving and enjoyable. With her well-earned reputation for being very much at home with children, she was irresistably drawn to these youngsters whose happiness

The Variety Club of Great Britain, which justly boasts of being the greatest children's charity in the world, had recently completed a massive fund-raising exercise to provide its famous Sunshine Coaches for the children of three schools in Bradford, Bristol and Seaford, Sussex. For handicapped children, outdoor activities are a vital part of the school curriculum and their first sight of their new means of indispensible transport arriving into Stable

depends so heavily on the goodwill of others. As she waved the last of the coaches off (above), their passengers carried with them special memories of their very royal day.

It all made for one of the happier and lighter sides of the otherwise very solemn, dignified and diplomatic character which traditionally surrounds the Court of St James's.

MAY 1982

A five-week season of Tchaikovsky's "Swan Lake," performed at the London Coliseum by the London Festival Ballet, came to a royal climax on 25th May when the Ballet's Patron, Princess Margaret, attended a gala performance in aid of its Development Fund. This new production by John Field was certain to attract the Princess' attention: she has maintained a lifelong interest in the ballet – she became the first President of the newly formed Royal Ballet in 1957 as part of her more general musical appreciation. Music and its interpretation in the wider arts have been important to her,

continued to be well aired in public, with less private matters again distinguished by varying degrees of controversy.

The publication in October of Nigel Dempster's biography "HRH The Princess Margaret: A Life Unfulfilled" contained a detailed résumé of material the author had previously disclosed in his *Daily Mail* gossip column, and more. It was said to have been read in draft and approved by the Princess, but her former husband, Lord Snowdon, dismissed it as having been "written without interviews." Jocelyn Stevens, a friend of the Princess, weighed in, detailing its many inaccuracies in an

as she disclosed in the BBC programme "Desert Island Discs" in 1981, when she selected favourite recordings of ballet music as well as jazz and opera.

Princess Margaret has, in the last twelve months, undertaken her usual quota of public engagements – including visits abroad to attend the Diamond Jubilee of King Sobhuza II of Swaziland in September, to confer independence in Antigua in November, and to open an art exhibition at Houston, Texas in February. But she will, if she cares to, remember it as a time when issues in her private life

article in the *Daily Express* – a paper which itself ran a week-long serialisation about her, in competition with the book's serialisation in the *Daily Mail*. The statement in the book that she "would like to marry again" seemed to be confirmed by the many sightings of her with the 55-year-old widower Norman Lonsdale. They were photographed together at a masked ball in November; he stayed with her on Mustique in February; and when the Princess was spotted wearing an unfamiliar ring on her engagement finger during an official visit to Glasgow in April, the rumour-mongers drew their

barred for the third time in four unhappy years from attending the Christmas Ball at Keele University of which she is Chancellor: nothing personal here; it was just that the left wingers in the Students' Union took objection to the police prowling around before and during royal visits. And she received her annual insult from Willie Hamilton MP who called her "a useless, middle-aged floozie" in front of 200 nurses and hospital workers as part of their campaign for higher pay. Sometimes she must wonder whether it's all worth it. Who'd be a Princess?

conclusions. They were almost actively encouraged by tantalisingly ambiguous statements by both Mr Lonsdale and the Princess' private secretary, but when two days later HRH turned up at an NSPCC lunch with *three* rings on her engagement finger, and unreserved denials were issued all round, the story magically vanished.

For good measure, the Princess was criticised quite severely for refusing – apparently on the grounds that it would spoil her hair-do – to wear a sterile hairnet at a medical products factory in Plymouth. She was

MAY 1982

The recently extended and refurbished showroom of Wedgwoods in Wigmore Street, London, opened by the Duke of Kent in February 1982, provided the setting for a short visit by the Duchess of Gloucester on 24th May. Her interest in music led her to be invited by the Editor of "Music Teacher" magazine to present the first ever awards for excellence in the field of teaching and learning music. "Music Teacher," the only publication of its kind, enlisted the help of a team of judges led by Sir David Willcocks, who

refreshment; their sponsorship was appropriate too since the winner of the 1981 Guinness Prize in the Young Musicians Platform of the South-East Arts Association, Ruth Faber, was present to introduce the proceedings with an unusual harp fanfare and to serenade the 100-strong gathering with music throughout the more informal interludes of the Duchess' visit. As Leonard Piercey, "Music Teacher's" editor, said: "There is a certain apt connection between Guinness and the harp." The awards presented by the

directed some of the music at last year's Royal Wedding and composed the new version of the National Anthem for it. Wedgwoods provided not only the premises on which the award ceremony was held, but also seven beautiful stained-glass coloured paperweights containing, appropriately, the figure of Tom the Piper, which were given to the award winners. Guinness provided the

Duchess, herself a pianist, represented many different kinds of achievement. Teachers, like Judith Burton (opposite page bottom left), one of two joint winners; pupils, like 14-year-old cellist Sean Gibbons, who once played a duet with Paul Tortellier; educational directors, and the media. In this last category, BBC South West TV won on the strength of their Music Quiz, while a special award went to Peter Hutchings, the producer of programmes for BBC Schools Radio.

In his introductory speech,

Leonard Piercey said he was gratified that the new Award Scheme had "more than justified our expectations" and the Duchess, following the presentations, praised the devotion of music teachers and eductionalists, the fruits of whose work are frequently gathered only in a long-term harvest. She pointed out how little concert audiences realise what labours by diligent teachers have gone into the artistry before them on the stage. After her speech (opposite page top centre) she chatted informally

with winners and judges, and with Ruth Faber (above and far left) who had provided that delightful background music. She left as quietly as she had arrived, though not without signing the visitors book first. "Birgitte 24.v.82" evidences the visit, in a bold upright hand, not many pages after one which reveals "Edward 9.2.82."

MAY 1982

On 5th April, three days after the Argentinians invaded the Falkland Islands, a 36-ship Task Force set out from British and Gibraltar ports on a mission to engage the invader, if necessary, in war. The operation was the largest of its kind since the Suez crisis of 1956 and the possibilities were unthinkable. Portsmouth disgorged a contingent of ships, including the 27,000-ton *HMS Hermes* (right), led by one of the Royal Navy's latest aircraft carriers *HMS Invincible* (bottom left). And on the *Invincible* was the Queen's second son, 22-year-old Prince Andrew.

It was at the end of January that Prince Andrew flew from RNAS Culdrose to join 47 other members of *Invincible's* 820 squadron at Portsmouth as a fully-fledged helicopter pilot, one of a dozen ratings flying Sea King helicopters. He went with impressive credentials, including the trophy for having gained the most flying marks of his class. And he was impressed with his new ship: "She's marvellous," he said at Rosyth in February. Plans affecting both him and the *Invincible* – a visit by the Queen in April and exercises in foreign waters in May – began to falter as the Falklands dispute loomed. On 2nd April Prince Andrew, like a thousand other ratings and officers, was called from leave – he was at Windsor Castle – to join the general alert after the Argentinians invaded.

There were hasty consultations with the Queen and Prince Philip as to whether he should

much to his frustration – against the possibility of his being killed or taken prisoner, while more recently the present Duke of Kent found himself being withdrawn from Northern Ireland after the shortest of spells with the British troops there in 1970; it was thought that he was too obvious a target for IRA lawlessness and that he would be in disproportionately greater danger than the ordinary soldier.

There were rumours that Prince Andrew would resign if barred from sailing, but he need not

be allowed, or compelled, to go. The precedents were unhelpful. Prince Andrew's grandfather, King George VI, served at the Battle of Jutland and came back unscathed; his great-uncle Lord Mountbatten captained the *Kelly* and was lucky to survive its bombing by German Stukas; another great-uncle, the late Duke of Kent served in the RAF during the Second World War and was killed when his aircraft crashed in Scotland during a mission north. Against that, the Duke of Windsor's military activities during the First World War were severely curtailed – have feared. For the Queen there was no question of his being withheld and for his commanding officer no question of special treatment: "Prince Andrew is a serving officer and will do whatever is required of him. He's a member of my crew and flies like any other man. That's the way we play it."

So to the accompaniment of cheering crowds, massed bands, an escort of helicopters and bursts of red flares, the *Invincible,* 19,500 tons of anti-submarine cruiser, commissioned in 1980 and already under contract for sale to the Australians for £175 million, led the fleet of ships out of Portsmouth harbour. The three-week, 8,000 mile journey was made in seas described as "rough to bloody" as the southern hemisphere's winter approached, and put into perspective any complaints the Prince may have voiced about the ducking he got when the ship crossed the line.

Meanwhile, his approach was being ridiculed by the Argentinian newspaper "Cronica" who called him "the Crown Prince of Colonialism" who "should have brought his nappies with him."

'H', as Prince Andrew was known to his squadron, drilled with the rest of them throughout. Each

day he collected his pistol, broke in his flak-jacket, studied enemy ships and prepared for the inevitable onslaught. His blooding was not long following. On 24th April he flew out to rescue a crewman from the *Hermes* whose helicopter was lost. A week or so later he was flying over the wreck of *HMS Sheffield,* the first major casualty of an undeclared war. And from that point on he was out round

the clock, flying low over the waters round the *Invincible,* acting as decoy for the lethal Exocet missiles which had scuppered the *Sheffield.* He was as vulnerable as anyone in the conflict that killed over 250 Britons.

He spent a hundred days at sea, and faced another hundred in and around the Falkland Islands, in readiness for any subsequent exigencies – the trouble with an undeclared war is that no-one can be quite sure when peace has definitely arrived – before *Invincible's* return to home waters in September.

His brother, Prince Charles, whose naval career ended five years before, admitted that he would not like to have been in the South Atlantic. On 25th May he, as Elder Brother of Trinity House, accompanied the Duke of Edinburgh as Master, in the happier business of attending the annual Court and Church Service. These pictures show them in procession from Trinity House where the Court was held, to St Olave's Church, in the City of London.

On 27th May, a welcome splash of colour on a drab day was provided by the comings and goings at Westminster Abbey where the Queen installed the latest crop of Knights Grand

is cocooned in time and place. In time, it is a comparatively short ritual surrounded by a grandiose religious service full of trumpetings, psalms of praise, patriotic music and the constant shifting of beadles, almsmen, genealogists and Scarlet Rod. In place, it happens in the inner sanctum of the Order's own chapel, the King Henry VII Chapel, away from the eyes of established Knights in the body of the Abbey.

Like most occasions of high ceremony, precision is of the essence. Gentlemen at Arms and Yeomen of the Guard officially took up positions at 10.57 am; Princess Alice arrived (bottom, far right and opposite page bottom left) with her lady in waiting Miss Jane Egerton-Warburton at 11.05; Prince Charles – Grand Master since

Cross of the Order of the Bath. As Sovereign of the Order she presided at this irregularly-staged embodiment of a tradition formalised in 1725. For, unlike the Garter Service, this is not an annual event: this year's ceremony was held to install those Knights appointed since 1978. There were eleven of them – five generals, four air marshals, an admiral and Lord Adeane, the Queen's former private secretary. Fortunately for all of them the bathing rite, from which the Order takes its title, has long since been dropped, though George I included it in the schedule of obligatory ceremonies on creating the Order out of the old medieval "Degree of Knighthood."
The installation ceremony itself

who, as Grand Master, delivers it to the Senior of the Knights to be installed, so that they can all take the oath. This includes an undertaking to "defend maidens, widows and orphans in their rights and . . . suffer no extortion."

The Grand Master has then to seat the new Knights in their

stalls, but no sooner is this done than they have to rise again to go and stand beneath their respective banners.

Another pattern of synchronised movement precedes the Queen's obeisance before the altar as she offers gold and silver, as does the senior of the new Knights. There follows a ritual drawing and sheathing of swords, and exhortations to defend the Gospel and maintain the "Sovereign's Right and Honour," before the select gathering returns to rejoin the congregation.

A general thanksgiving and prayers are followed by the Blessing and the National Anthem, and the procession out through the East Cloister begins (left and far left). And a few words from the Queen and Prince Charles (opposite page) to a cluster of school-children convinces them that these robed and tiara'd figures with their magical symbols are pleasantly human after all.

1975 – arrived (left) at 11.09; and the Queen (far right) at 11.12.

The service takes much the same form as any Morning Service, with psalm, lesson, versicles and responses, prayers and anthems. Then a thin procession of royalty and Knights moves up the Abbey past the High Altar and into the King Henry VII Chapel, while anthems are sung. Once inside the Chapel the members of the procession take their appointed places – the Queen and Prince Charles have special stalls – and sit, except for the Knights about to be installed, who remain standing. Bath King of Arms receives a Book of Statutes from the Deputy Secretary and proceeds towards Prince Charles

MAY 1982

There is nothing particularly new about the Queen of the United Kingdom meeting the Holy Father. Elizabeth II has met a succession of Popes – as Princess Elizabeth she was received by Pope Pius XII, and as Queen she called on Pope John XXIII in 1961, and on the present Pope in 1980 during each of her State Visits to Italy. Since Henry VIII broke with the Church of Rome, however, no

Pope has ever set foot inside the United Kingdom, far less parleyed with the Sovereign. For that reason His Holiness' forty minutes with Her Majesty at Buckingham Palace on 28th May was one of the most historically significant events of her reign. As a meeting between Heads of State it was all a matter of ordinary diplomatic courtesy, but as a symbol of the coming together of two churches, whose rupture over four hundred years ago still excites powerful controversy, it had a potency all its own.

That was particularly so in the light of further controversy stirred up by news of his impending visit: the Orange Order branded the Queen as a potential "traitor to the Constitution" and Mr Enoch Powell said it was "constitutionally and logically impossible for England to contain both the Queen and the Pope." Then further difficulties arose with the Falklands crisis, the Argentinians claiming that the visit would bestow the unfair advantage of Papal blessing upon the British cause.

This led to a further confusion. Originally, to appease the ultra-

Protestants it had been stated that the meeting was not between Heads of Churches but between Heads of State. When the Falklands crisis became an issue the Argentinians were told that the meeting had no political, but only a religious, significance.

The Pope mollified the Argentinians by promising to visit them in June, and his tour of Britain and meeting with the Queen passed off quietly and satisfactorily. The Pope was met at the Palace by an official (far left) but the Queen came out to the Grand Entrance to bid him farewell personally.

JUNE 1982

Just prior to the running of the 200th Derby on 6th June 1979, the Queen sent a simply-worded, but obviously profoundly sincere message to the Chairman of United Racecourses Ltd, Mr Evelyn de Rothschild: "The Derby is the most famous event in the world's racing calendar and I send my very best wishes for a very successful bicentenary." And, she added: "I shall look forward to being present again – Elizabeth R."

That last sentence almost need not have been added. The Royal Family as a whole are staunch supporters of the event and show every likelihood of remaining so for at least the next

and sisters began to follow his example and by the end of his own reign, royalty attended the Derby regularly.

Queen Victoria had little taste for Epsom's annual beanfeast. Her serious-minded consort encouraged her to reserve her patronage for serious-minded matters, and her own scorn for the worldly follies of her discreditable uncles, including George IV, made the Prince Consort's job easy. Her moral and religious scruples would also have been outraged by the story, if she ever heard it, that early in her reign a Sussex parson had, in the course of Morning Service, intoned a prayer which

generation or two. But British royalty have always been connected in one degree or another with the scene, which until the mid-nineteenth century had been enjoyed almost wholly and solely by the landed aristocracy – the Grosvenors, the Bedfords, the Rutlands and the Graftons – and by a smattering of well-heeled top brass from

the Army and Royal Navy. As Prince of Wales, the Prince Regent (later King George IV) showed considerable enthusiasm almost from the start – indeed his horse, Sir Thomas, won the ninth Derby in 1788 – and although his interest was intensely personal, and disapproved of by his father George III, many of his brothers

he introduced as "the collect for the Sunday before the Derby." It was after the marriage of her eldest son, the future King Edward VII, and the brilliant court which he and his consort, later Queen Alexandra, held at the apex of London Society in the late nineteenth century, that royal patronage of the Derby really took off. In the earlier

landowners, bankers, foreign aristocrats and the *nouveau-riche* – with the glories and excitement of what was by then a well-established racing tradition.

The Prince's boost to the Epsom Derby was, eventually, well-rewarded. In 1892 he sent his mare Perdita II to be mated with St Simon, a stallion whose brilliant career, in all but the Derby, made him an expensive and much sought-after stud. The result was Persimmon, a colt who showed no promise at all until the very minute he arrived at Epsom in 1896. He amazed all by winning the

Derby win – almost equally unexpected, since the jockey was an untried stable-lad – with Diamond Jubilee, and it was a fitting finale to his short reign that the last Derby the King saw, in 1909, was won by his horse Minoru.

Since then the good fortune of winning the Derby has escaped the Royal Family – ironically throughout a period of keenest and most prolonged interest and most frequent and regular attendance. The "near misses" – King George V's Anmer was felled when the suffragette protester Emily Davison threw herself under him at Tattenham

years this was not so much because of the Prince of Wales' direct involvement, but because it was he who introduced a whole new section of international Society into the field of breeding thoroughbreds and racing them on English racecourses. His own brother, the Duke of Connaught, was a keen *aficionado,* as was his son

and eventual successor, King George V. Foreign royalty – in particular the Princess of Wales' Russian in-laws – took an increasing interest in the English racing scene and encouraged similar events in their own countries. And the Prince of Wales was also responsible for acquainting many of his wealthy and influential friends –

Derby in a thrilling finish, and Begg's water-colour of the Prince leading him into the winner's enclosure epitomises, perhaps idealises, the ecstatic popular acclaim. Persimmon went on to win the St Leger, the Ascot Gold Cup and the Eclipse Stakes.

In the year before his accession, Edward VII achieved another

Corner in 1913, and the present Queen's Aureole, beaten only by the dream-like performance of the famous Pinza in 1953 – have been bitter disappointments, but the Queen and her family were at Epsom in 1981 (opposite) and in 1982 (this page) and will doubtless be there again in 1983. One year her luck will change.

JUNE 1982

"Buckingham Palace – June 2: The Queen accompanied by the Duke of Edinburgh, Queen Elizabeth the Queen Mother, Princess Anne Mrs Mark Phillips, The Duke and Duchess of Gloucester, Prince and Princess Michael of Kent and Princess Alexander (sic) the Hon Mrs Angus Ogilvy and the Hon Mr Angus Ogilvy, honoured Epsom Races with her presence today."

It's a bit of a mouthful, even for the Court Circular, but as usual it relates only the bare facts of attendance or presence, and in this case without the additional details of how they all got there, what they did when they arrived, or how they travelled back. But

breed and race a Derby winner still continues, has rarely missed this most prestigious of the world's classic races and the most financially rewarding of the British classics. And it is a rare occasion when the majority of the Royal family do not accompany her.

more conservatively, wore her complete outfit of matching hat, coat and dress. Princess Anne was in a fresh, green dress, while the Duchess of Gloucester preferred bright white. Princess Michael at Epsom was indistinguishable from Princess Michael at Royal Ascot, with her stately

of arms or crowns affixed to their roofs. It was sudden and violent, as if to remind everyone who had come to enjoy this annual beano that the Falklands were closer than they might have thought. It sent some 300,000 people scurrying for shelter – girls in bikinis or ra-ras looked

then everyone knows that the Royal Family habitually have a ripping time at Epsom – it's almost as imperative as solemnity at the Opening of Parliament or hats at Ascot. The Queen, whose quest to

This year the Queen arrived coatless – unusually for her but the weather in the first week of June had for once turned up trumps and the sun beat down relentlessly for most of the afternoon. The Queen Mother,

ensemble and grand feathered hat.

A thunderstorm broke just after the impressive royal arrival – a procession of Rolls Royces purring up the course with badges displaying personal coats

never so out of place beneath picnic rugs and newspapers, and grown men, stripped to the waist and covered in sun tan oil, cowered under the nearest umbrellas.

An hour before the big race it all

stopped and the sun rejuvenated the festival atmosphere. Eventually the Royal party came down from the stand and inspected the 1982 Derby runners from the side of the course (bottom picture, the Queen Mother and the Queen with – left to right – Mr Ogilvy, Princess Alexandra, Prince Philip and – at the back in the centre – the Duke of Gloucester). As the expressions on the royal faces made clear, all were fascinated by the procession of these finely groomed horses cantering by at the peak of their fitness and form. They returned to the Royal Box where their every

The Queen had a cup of tea there and made a close inspection of the contents of the flower box. The 1982 Derby was as exciting, both in anticipation and on the day itself, as almost any of the two hundred-odd meetings of past years. The prize to the eventual winner was higher than ever, and the value in international stud fees would be phenomenal. Yet, for once, there were no royal histrionics or the customary excited gesticulations as the runners came home. The Queen's personal interest seemed more dispassionate than in previous years. Perhaps that was because, in the hour of war, Peacetime only came seventh.

gesture could be watched: Princess Anne discussed with her father (opposite page, left), the Queen with her mother (opposite page, right) and Princess Michael with everyone (above and centre pictures).

Or perhaps because, as Susan Sangster's horse Golden Fleece ran in the winner, the Queen knew she had yet another year to wait before her chance came up again.

JUNE 1982

The Prince and Princess of Wales were back at Broadlands on 29th May to attend a huge private party hosted by Lord and Lady Romsey to raise money for the United World Colleges, of which Lord Mountbatten was president. The occasion was not strictly an official one, though with 450 guests to shake hands with, it might have seemed like one.

On the following day they both went to Smith's Lawn, Windsor, where Prince Charles, now heavily committed each weekend to the new polo season, was to play for Les Diables Bleus (The Blue Devils) in the first round of the Queen's

Cup. Prince Charles arrived earlier by himself to attend a pre-match briefing. The Queen herself arrived from Windsor Castle – where she spends most weekends – and made for the new £30,000 Royal Box, where the Princess of Wales, who showed up last of all, joined her. But not for long. During the match, the Princess left the Royal Box to greet a friend, and became involved in conversation with some of the other spectators, drinking Pimms No 1 and sitting on the bonnet of Prince Charles' sports car. Prince Charles' team won 8-6 in that game but fortune eluded him on 31st May when he

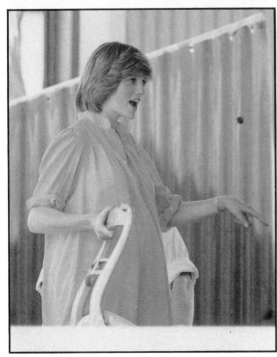

returned to Smith's Lawn to play for the Canadian team Maple Leaf against the local side Eaglesfield. The Prince began well enough by scoring a goal, but half way through one of the chukkas there was a scramble in the goalmouth in which, closely marking his opposite number, he was involved. Eaglesfield's Alex Bamberg took a swing at the ball, and in the follow-through his mallet ricochetted off another player's mallet and struck Prince Charles in the mouth. The Prince galloped off the field, shouting to his new stud groom, Raoul Correa, for water. Correa mistook his request and thought he wanted to change his pony, but eventually a bottle of Malvern water was brought to him and he was able to return to the game as the chukka was resumed.

He looked dazed throughout the rest of the match, which was watched by 1,500 spectators, and found afterwards that his lip had been split and one of his eye teeth had come loose. But he did not need any medical treatment, though he nursed a bruise for the rest of the week. Fortunately he had been wearing a visor, which he had adopted after being trampled on by a pony in 1980: his left cheek still shows the scar from that accident.

The Princess of Wales did not see her husband's latest mishap – she was at Highgrove – but she was not discouraged from watching him play polo again the next week. Remembering how often she had winced at seeing him being tackled in matches the previous year, many people thought that another physical injury, however minor, would put the Princess off the game for good.

But she took the opportunity to nail the myth of her antipathy. When she arrived at Smith's Lawn again on 4th June (these and previous pages) she told the Press: "I don't know why people think I dislike polo. I love the game. That's why I'm here." She had travelled in her new car, to be greeted by Prince Charles and his polo manager, Major Ronald Ferguson (opposite page, centre picture).

At 84°F it was another boiling hot day and Prince Charles was again playing for Les Diables Bleus, in the second round of the Queen's Cup. This time he succeeded in completing the match without injury and celebrated his team's victory by offering his wife a sweet before they both hopped into their car to leave (below left).

The victory of Les Diables Bleus that afternoon qualified them for the finals, but their luck ran out next day, the 5th June when, in front of the Queen (overleaf) who was, naturally, present to award her Cup, they had to be content with runner-up status. The Prince received a finalist's Cup on behalf of his

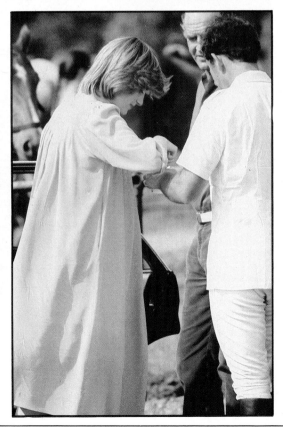

team, and handed it to his wife as the royal party left the presentation area.

The Princess, who wore an attractive green polka-dotted dress, was with Prince Charles as he made his way back to his car. Here he met Sarah Ferguson, the daughter of his polo manager, who had companioned the Princess during part of the match (p. 209 wearing blue) and gave her a spontaneous hug and a kiss. His wife pretended to object and for a moment seemed to alarm both the Prince and her friend by the seriousness of her complaint. But she couldn't keep a straight face for long enough, and Prince Charles rewarded her with a kiss and playfully ruffled her hair.

This was one of the last public appearances the Princess of Wales made before the birth of her baby and she might justifiably have looked back on it all with a degree of satisfaction. It had been a public, almost as

soon as it had been a private fact, that she was with child, and the very public interest must have made it an extremely long pregnancy indeed.

Though it began in a glow of public congratulation – the Lord Mayor of London likened the news to a hallmark on the gold ingot of the Royal Wedding, and the Prince of Wales praised "the wonderful effect my dear wife has had on everyone" – excesses of publicity threatened at times to turn the whole thing sour and cause the mother-to-be to modify her flexible, informal approach to her royal duties. Over-zealous photographers plagued her at Highgrove and Tetbury and again on the

Bahamian holiday, and were rebuked by the Queen for doing so. Even the BBC was considered to have gone too far with a comedy sketch showing the Princess giving evidence in a court case against a contraceptive firm. Rumours abounded that American and British firms were in the process of making feature films about her courtship with the Prince of Wales, one of them containing "details not revealed before," but we have yet to see any finished results.

Artists had a field day. Bryan Organ's official painting of the Princess was slashed at the National Portrait Gallery, where it now hangs restored and protected by Perspex. The wedding was celebrated on canvas by Sue Ryder, who portrayed the Princess in a froth of light, filmy bridal silk, but avoiding over-sentimentality. Ruskin Spear painted the Prince

and Princess kissing on Buckingham Palace balcony, but over-emphasised what was in reality a fleeting peck almost into a clinch. Carol Payne went one worse and exhibited a painting at Plymouth showing

the royal couple in more intimate surroundings.

The speculation about twins must have sickened her at times. The baby's sex was universally discussed and the general plumping for a boy proved

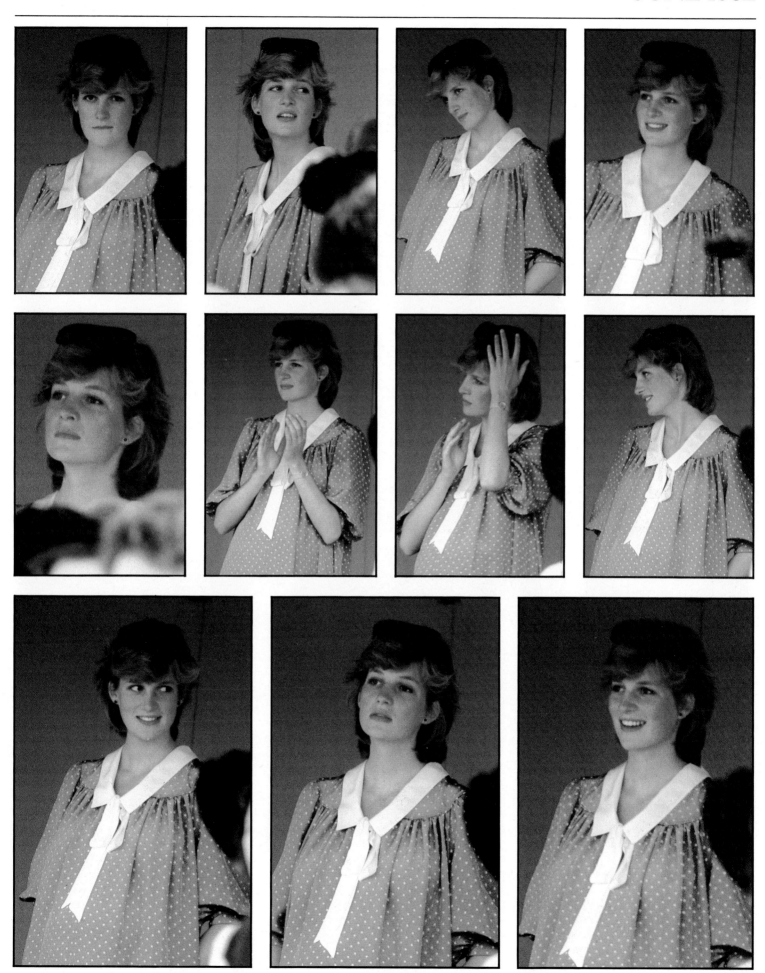

inspired. The place of its birth divided the country – Highgrove, Buckingham Palace and St Mary's Paddington were all candidates. The suppliers of baby clothes, maternity wear, nursery furniture, equipment and toys, became the target of endless Press detective work. (Incidentally, the doll trade was

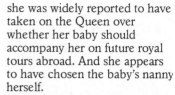

she was widely reported to have taken on the Queen over whether her baby should accompany her on future royal tours abroad. And she appears to have chosen the baby's nanny herself.

If one thing is totally beyond doubt it is that the codes of public behaviour as they affect

thrilled: "This is definitely the year of the baby doll," said one manufacturer.) Even the Princess' own bedroom, with the chance of housing a four-poster bed more than once slept in by the French courtesan, Diane de Poitiers, excited interest.

If ever the Princess had properly acquired an image, it changed over this period. She seemed less vulnerable than before her marriage and rumours that she was decisive, unyielding, even precociously ambitious began to spread. Certainly photographers caught her more than once letting everyone know of some displeasure. In five months she was held responsible for having sacked Prince Charles' valet and two of her own detectives and

princes and princesses of the Blood Royal and their spouses have changed fundamentally and irrevocably. From the relative obscurity of a position as the youngest daughter of an Earl, the Princess has become the wife of the heir to the Throne, but she has brought to the monarchy as an institution all the best elements of uninhibited social and personal behaviour. It raised eyebrows at first, this free and easy chat with the common herd, this touching of other people's babies, those giggling larks with young children. But no chord with the public was more sympathetically struck, and no more timely boost to the

monarchy's popularity was ever so comprehensively furnished or maintained. And all, it seems, without effort.

That statement may imply that it is easy to "become" a member of the Royal Family and to assimilate its ways, its taboos, its "image." That may or may not be the case – only the Princess herself and her mentor Lady Susan Hussey can verify, and for obvious reasons they are not available for comment. It probably comes nearer the truth to say that the Princess has modified what everybody thought was the fixed, unchanging manner of royalty whenever it appeared in public. If so she is accomplishing this not through perversity or even as the result of a conscious decision. She has clearly accepted Prince Charles' hand in marriage and the monarchy's soul for life on terms which reflect her own uncomplicated values as much as the institution's complexities and quaintness. The public have been easily won over, and the Royal Family is demonstrably not far behind.

JUNE 1982

to introduce young people from the age of 13 to 23 to a whole range of challenging activities which, as suburb-bound Londoners, they may not have considered feasible.

The event lasted for seven hours and Prince Charles, who admits to being a Capital Radio listener, spent almost two hours there himself. Still showing the last traces of the split lip he had received at polo the previous week (opposite page, far right), he was taken on an extensive and detailed tour of a dozen or so of the total of 95 different sport and leisure opportunities on show.

There was no shortage of choice, and the sheer width of

Sunday is not a day on which any member of the Royal Family entertains invitations to undertake engagements, but the odd exception has proved the rule. Any project to help or encourage young people is a good candidate for Prince Charles' support, and when that project aims at incorporating handicapped youngsters within its ambitions, the no-work-on-Sunday rule is worth breaking. On 6th June, the explorer Linda Batt-Rawden was one of two organisers who welcomed Prince Charles to Capital Radio's Venture Day, which was her own idea, at Battersea Park. It was the first of its kind, designed by the London-based radio station

activity available would have astounded the most optimistic hopes: pot-holing and archaeology, martial arts and first aid, sailing and hot-air ballooning – all were proved to be within the geographical and financial range of the majority of enthusiasts.

He saw a competition based on BBC TV's "It's a Knockout," but organised between mixed teams of able-bodied and handicapped people, and designed to show that "disabled" is not synonymous with "incompetent." He watched a small-scale firing range, set up by the Territorial Army, in action, and inspected a mock-up of an archaeological dig; this was doubly interesting for the Prince not only because of his wide knowledge of the subject, in which he graduated at Cambridge in 1970, but also because the display was erected by the Wandsworth Historical Society, whose Vice-President is the Princess of Wales' father, Earl Spencer.

As a sometime go-kart enthusiast, Prince Charles was keen to hear about the latest developments from a group of children from the South London based Oasis Karting Project (opposite page, top left), and in particular to inspect one of the five karts on show that was specially adapted for disabled drivers. His experiences with an

old lady called Mary Rose gave him plenty to talk about at the sub-aqua stand (opposite page, top right).

Perhaps his chance encounter with 23-year-old Margaret Mundle (opposite page, bottom pictures) provided the greatest impromptu fun of the day. She is the leader of the Classical Black reggae band, in which she plays the guitar, and she was wearing one of the skimpiest outfits of the day. But Prince Charles is of course the perfect gentleman and told her that he liked "whatever that is you're wearing" and commented cheerfully on the extraordinary height of the heels on her boots.

He spotted a three-man tandem

and asked to ride it along to his next port of call, which was Radio Lollipop, a hospital radio station for children.

The tandem, specially designed to help the blind and the mentally handicapped, was a great success as Prince Charles accorded it royal patronage. He was wedged in between two other riders who whisked him off to Radio Lollipop in what its disc-jockeys might call record time. In doing which he showed he was game for anything – as the Venture Day intended.

JUNE 1982

Five years ago to the day, Britain was in the grip of the Queen's Silver Jubilee celebrations. On 7th June 1982 the country watched the unfolding of one of those perennial chapters of the Queen's reign which have given it its distinctive character. It was another in a long line of "firsts," for just over a week after Pope John Paul II had been the first Pontiff to meet the Sovereign on British soil, Ronald Reagan, the fortieth President of the United States of America, became the first to be welcomed as a guest of the Queen at Windsor. It was an interesting triangular coincidence that the President and the Pope had met in Rome immediately before the visit to Windsor.

Due to arrive at Heathrow Airport at six o'clock in the evening, the President was almost half an hour late, owing to an industrial dispute at Rome Airport. But Prince Philip, looking somewhat incongruous in morning suit, waited, casting his eyes skyward for signs of the aircraft or looking around him at the charmless views of the cargo terminal on one side and the quarantine quarters on the other.

A blue and white Boeing 707, officially named "Presidential Air Force One," flew into sight and an army of police marksmen on top of buildings and ringing the tarmac, settled into position. Twelve of Britain's crack marksmen and a large contingent of the President's 150 bodyguards were amongst them.

The landing was good, and the President, in dark blue suit and red tie, emerged hearty and smiling to a warm, genial greeting from the Queen's husband (pictures below). Mrs Reagan, on her second trip to Britain – the first was for the Royal Wedding – looked thrilled to be here again.

The Prince and his guests spent a few minutes chatting together before the President, waving and giving the thumbs-up to admirers on top of the airport building, was brought to the line of ministerial celebrities, led by the Prime Minister. After five minutes of formal presentations, Prince Philip led the President and his lady back to where a couple of American Marine Corps Sea King helicopters were waiting. They boarded one of them, and accompanied by the reserve machine and by two dull-green escort helicopter gunships, choppered off for Windsor.

The Queen had received the signal that her guests were on their way and, wearing a bright yellow outfit, was ready and waiting on the lawns just outside the private apartments of the

Castle. With her, formally dressed, like his father, was the Prince of Wales. The Presidential helicopter landed safely and its three august occupants stepped out (below centre) and marched across the lawn (right and far right) for the historic meeting with the Queen and her heir (below). There was a short bow from Mr Reagan, but no curtsey from his wife, for the Queen. Mrs Reagan

had too often been on the receiving end of criticism back home for bending the knee to royalty and had decided to repeat the attitude she had adopted for her visit in 1981 – a cordial handshake but not a single deferential gesture. The conversations were brief: there were official ceremonies to be got through. The party walked up the steps to the sunken garden against the East Terrace of the Castle, and through the Chester Tower to

the Quadrangle – very much the inner sanctum of the Queen's private residence. At 200 yards long and eighty wide it is big enough to accommodate a sizeable reception committee, and it was there in the form of the 1st Battalion Grenadier Guards.
The Queen led the President, while Prince Philip, Mrs Reagan and Prince Charles followed, to the East Wall of the Quadrangle where a carpet marked the saluting base, and their arrival

JUNE 1982

was greeted with the rousing strains of the British and American national anthems (top right). As it happened, Mrs Reagan was out of line: protocol demanded that the Queen and the President should stand level with each other, but that their respective spouses should be a pace or two back. Prince Philip, who should know the ropes by now, complied as if it all came naturally, but Mrs Reagan stepped forward at the last moment, hand reverently on her heart as the band played. The Queen tried unsuccessfully to put things right without being obtrusive but gave up as Prince Philip resignedly shrugged his shoulders.

gave a private dinner for her guests in the State dining room. Having met the Queen Mother, the Princess of Wales, Princess Anne and Captain Mark Phillips, they sat down to a meal of fillet of haddock, breasts of chicken stuffed with mangoes, and raspberry jam-filled

Prince Philip then escorted Mr Reagan over to the lines of Guardsmen for the Presidential inspection of the guard of honour (right and top centre), and a march-past (below centre) followed their return to where the Queen and Prince Charles were waiting with Mrs Reagan. Prince Philip returned to provide her with some company as the parade passed them (right and below right). Then, the formalities over, the entire party moved off towards the private apartments.
Again, protocol was the victim. Instead of walking with the Queen, the President motioned his wife to go first – "It's an old Reagan family custom," said his Press Secretary afterwards. But by then nobody seemed to mind these understandable lapses and the short journey through the Sovereign's Entrance past the splendidly-dressed Military Knights, proceeded on its way. Shortly afterwards the Queen

pancakes with whipped cream. All with the necessary liquid refreshment – white wine, a Chateau Batailley claret, champagne and vintage port. The President left the Castle that evening to attend a reception at the American Embassy in London and was greeted by a noisy demonstration from 2,000 people, including fifty MPs, protesting against America's "nuclear madness" and her support of some right-wing South American regimes. "He is not," said the demonstration's leader, "welcome in this country." An earlier demonstration by eighty women,

who blockaded the Stock Exchange in protest against cruise missiles in Britain, resulted in eleven arrests. It all contrasted strangely with the Royal Horse Artillery's gun salute in Hyde Park as the President had stepped from his aircraft onto British soil that evening.

The President and his wife slept that night in the Lancaster Tower of the Castle, overlooking the famous Long Walk into Home Park. Their suite included two bedrooms, hung with portraits of long-dead royal ancestors, two bathrooms, a dressing room dotted with miniatures and a drawing room containing salmon-pink sofas and chairs, and draped with Victorian-embroidered cream curtains. A gallery of Stubbses and Canelettos encrusted the connecting corridors.

By seven the next morning the visitors were awake: perhaps earlier if the sound of aircraft

approaching Heathrow Airport had disturbed them. "We're used to it," the President told the Queen. "Our home is right by the National Airport in Washington. We have the same problem." Be that as it may, there was a light breakfast of bacon and eggs before they were whisked off to the Royal Mews, where a special royal ride was to begin.

A dispassionate observer of the arrangements negotiated between the Royal Household and the White House in respect of this hour-long diversion might be forgiven for imagining that it was one of the greatest and most significant sixty minutes of the present millennium, and certainly bigger and better than anything seen either in Mr Reagan's days in Hollywood or on the battlefield at Dettingen where King George II became the last British monarch to lead

natural light to dispense with the need for floodlighting. And ultimately the army of bodyguards and security advisers was whittled down to a mere platoon.

In this spirit of Anglo-American compromise, the Queen's long-maintained love for life in the saddle, and the President's equally long experience of it on the film sets of Hollywood, came together that morning in a gentle, hour-long ride through Windsor's glistening parkland. The Queen had chosen her 8-year-old horse Centennial – a gift from the Canadian Mounties – for the President, since he was "a nice, obedient horse" with a reputation for being staid and eminently manageable. In fact the President found him a little frisky and struggled at times to keep him on a short rein. The Queen, riding her 20-year-old mare Burmese (left), had no such trouble. The horse had come through last year's

his army into battle.

For a Presidential delegation had visited Windsor earlier in the year to finalise security arrangements and had, it is reported, attempted to turn the entire episode into a pictorial extravaganza. They detailed the way they would like the Queen to ride, hoped that the shrubbery in the Long Walk could be suitably floodlit, and insisted on an accompanying posse of security men. In nearly all respects their requests were not met, the Queen feeling that the normal arrangements for photographers and film crews would, subject to some minor concessions, be sufficient and that there would be enough

Trooping drama with flying colours: this was a piece of cake. Neither the Queen nor the President wore helmets, and so provoked adverse comment, implied or expressed, from the Pony Club, the Jockey Club and the Royal Society for the Prevention of Accidents. The Queen herself would have had some comment, it seemed, on the President's banter with Pressmen who bellowed questions at him which he felt compelled to answer as the Queen waited impatiently for him to get on with the ride. Behind them, separated only by a Range Rover full of detectives, came Prince Philip, indulging in a spot of four-in-hand driving to

cause in the Falklands by congratulating him on "putting freedom on the offensive, where it ought to be." The President responded by calling her "foreseeing and courageous, returning her country's people to the roots of their strength with the eloquence and determi-

give Mrs Reagan a more sedate means of transport.

It was back to business and the President returned to the Castle to prepare for a working lunch at No 10 Downing Street, where he was met by Mrs Thatcher in a ceremony at the front door (above). In her speech of welcome she made a point of implying her appreciation of his ultimate support for Britain's

nation necessary to lead."
The same sentiments emerged
at a scintillating State banquet
held in St George's Hall at
Windsor Castle that night,
(these pages) at which the entire
adult complement of the Royal
Family were present – except the
Princess of Wales and the Queen
Mother, who was away on her
annual tour of the Channel
Ports. The royal ladies glittered
in their magnificent assortment
of tiaras, and the gentlemen
glowed in their Windsor uniform
with the bright red collars and
cuffs ordained by King George
III.
After dinner – Balmoral salmon,
lamb in Madeira sauce with
spinach, cauliflower and
croquette potatoes, followed by
strawberries and cream with
meringue – the Queen formally
welcomed the President in a
speech which confirmed the
mutual admiration in which the
two countries held each other:
"Our commitment to a common
cause has led us to fight in two
World Wars and to continue to

stand together in defence of
freedom."
Then with a bluntness which
could only have been prompted
by a Prime Minister knowing
her country was on the verge of
victory in the South Atlantic, the
Queen turned to the Falkland
Islands. "These past weeks," she
said, "have been testing ones for
this country, when once again we
have had to stand up for the
cause of freedom. The conflict
was thrust on us by naked
aggression and we are naturally
proud of the way our fighting
men are serving their country.
But throughout the crisis we
have drawn comfort from the
understanding shown by the
American people. We have
admired the honesty, patience
and skill with which you have
performed your dual role as ally
and intermediary. In return we
can offer an understanding of
how hard it is to bear the
daunting responsibilities of
world power."
The President in reply took the
opportunity to review his own

stand on questions involving
world power, and spoke on
Poland, the Soviet Union,
terrorism and the Middle East.
Significantly he implied his
continued support for Britain in
the Falklands: "Young men are
fighting not for mere real estate
but for the belief that aggression
must not pay. Together,
committed to the preservation of
freedom and our way of life, we
must strengthen a weakening
international order."
His speech, which a dozen of his
staff had sweated over for weeks
previously, and to which the
President had himself added the
final flourishes less than forty-
eight hours before, distilled the
essence of his country's
justification for remaining aloof
from the politics of the Falklands
conflict – even-handed, they
called it at the time – until the
gloves were off. Britain was
critical then, but relations were
now at their friendliest as the
Queen presided over this
glittering formal reconciliation.

JUNE 1982

If truth be told it was not actually completed until 1692 but the 66 acres of land were bought in 1682 and work on the institution "for the relief of such Land Souldiers . . . lame or infirme in the Service of the Crowne" began the same year. Its full name, the Royal Hospital, derives from its founding by King Charles II, the "Merry Monarch," whose restoration in 1660 led the monarchist, and in events somewhat reactionary, backlash against the austerities of Puritan Britain.

The annual parade has for decades enjoyed royal patronage

Thursday 10th June 1982 was a day of anniversaries. Eight years before, the Duke of Gloucester, the last surviving child of King George V, died. It was also Prince Philip's sixty-first

birthday: guns boomed again in Hyde Park and at the Tower; flags fluttered brightly from public buildings. Which was nice because it was also the day on which the Queen, as a special mark of her affection for the Chelsea Pensioners, chose to celebrate with them the three hundredth anniversary of the founding of their Hospital.

and this special royal visit added calibre and a grand sense of occasion to the colourful vision of the lines of red-coated in-pensioners (above) and the Romanesque statue of "our Pious Founder," swathed in oak leaves (top left) as a reminder of his hiding place after the Battle of Worcester in 1651. Figure Court was alive with the shuffle

of scarlet, the winking of a thousand medals, the brisk pacings of commanding officers in black, and the gentler sociable movements of the Queen. Dressed in a soft mauve outfit that was to become a favourite this summer, she reviewed 436 men, the able-bodied during the marchpast (above) and the others sitting on benches, black tricornes nodding and walking-sticks wagging as they hoped for the chance of a word with the Queen as she passed (right and below right).

It is a sobering thought that at 99 years of age, one of them could claim to have served in the Boer War in the last dim glimmer of the reign of her great-great-grandmother Queen Victoria. Others took part in campaigns in India as far back as 1908. Over a hundred of the Hospital's present complement served in the First World War, and nearly 250 in the Second. The roll call of their foreign service recall Britain's inter-war

imperial interests – Palestine, Iraq, East Africa and Aden. Between them, the in-pensioners share no fewer than 250 gallantry medals and awards for outstanding service, from the Order of the British Empire to the Belgian Albert Medal. King Charles II's foundation of the Hospital grew out of his recognition of the importance of his army. He would be gratified by the knowledge that after three hundred years the Hospital, and the royal connection, were still thriving.

JUNE 1982

It was an emotional parade, though as uncompromisingly military as ever. The Falklands were in everyone's mind and the swaggering panache of the more splendid military music prompted proud applause as spontaneously as the massed bands' rendering of "The Day Thou Gavest, Lord, Is Ended" drew tears from those moved by the realisation that, for some mothers' sons in the South Atlantic, life's day had ended indeed.

The Queen and Princess Margaret watched the ceremony from a balcony. Prince Philip, accompanied by the loudly-

Prince Philip is not one to make a song and dance about his birthday, but he might have known that the Royal Marines would not pass up the opportunity to pay their own tribute to their Captain General when on the evening of 10th June he took the Salute at the Beating the Retreat ceremony on Horse Guards Parade.

Warden, and some of the other towns of Kent and Sussex. She came via Portsmouth, where she arrived on the Royal Yacht *Britannia* (below right). Dressed overall and flying the Queen Mother's personal standard (left) with the ensign and its own flag, the Royal Yacht's arrival brought huge crowds out to welcome the Queen Mother (opposite page) who had earlier saluted the *Queen Elizabeth 2* as the two ships passed in the Solent. The *QE2* was on her way back to Southampton where a magnificent welcome awaited her after her voyage as a troopship to the South Atlantic:

applauded General Sir Steuart Pringle, (opposite page, top right) burst into laughter as in their final number the bands played a medley of tunes including "Happy Birthday to You."

The following day Queen Elizabeth the Queen Mother returned to London from her three-day visit to the Cinque Ports, of which she is Lord

she was carrying 700 survivors from three ships, the *Ardent,* the *Antelope* and the *Coventry,* all sunk in battle.

The Queen Mother's own homecoming was more successful than the departure from Windsor on 8th June. Her helicopter broke down shortly after it took off, and had to make an emergency landing on Smith's Lawn. The Queen

Mother made her journey to Kent in an Andover from London Airport, where she had been driven by car. She was late for her engagements, two of which had to be cancelled, but the remainder of her tour – one which she has made annually since her installation as Lord Warden in 1979 – went without further mishap.

JUNE 1982

The phrase "London has never seen anything like it" has a timeless journalistic ring to it, and usually refers to some splendid ceremonial event, like the most recent example of the Prince and Princess of Wales' wedding, or a particularly scintillating festival or firework display. But on 12th June it could have been, and was, applied to the astonishing phenomenon of the continuous, vertical and extremely heavy rain which fell on a hitherto sunlit capital just before the Queen was due out to attend Trooping the Colour on Horse Guards Parade.

It started, almost literally without warning, at 10.30 am, just as the Queen emerged from the Inner Courtyard of Buckingham Palace to stand at its gates and watch the Household Brigades go by on their way to the Parade. It was amazing how obviously it took everybody by surprise. In the usual crowds, swelled by the memory of the dramatic events of last year's Trooping, there was instant chaos in the general rush for rainwear and a thousand

cameras became instantly waterlogged. Had the Queen been on foot she would doubtless have turned on a sixpence and made for the shelter of the building behind her. But she was mounted, sidesaddle, on her regular Trooping mare Burmese. What was more, she was flanked by

her husband, son and cousin, also on horseback, and the parade was already in motion. Everything was irretrievably geared for the next two hours. There was no question of going back for any reason.

Least of all to fetch a cape. The rain had come too late for the order to be given for coats to be

lines of the Horse Guards building, dream of the days when Churchill held wartime Court in the depths of the ivy-clad Citadel towards the opposite side of the parade ground. No-one gazed admiringly at the contrast between the gaudy brilliance of the flags of Commonwealth nations as they fluttered on tall masts lining the approach road, and the stark severity of the memorial to the five Guards formations which stood, facing the Horse Guards building, against the rich green backdrop of St James's Park with its elegant, glistening, dripping plane trees. One could only marvel at the patience and – for once the phrase is not clichéd – the sense of duty that kept these thin red lines of Guards and their 260 musicians upright and still in such appalling conditions. It may have seemed to those soldiers who stayed in England that winter in the Falkland

worn and already the Queen's soldiers, both at the Palace and waiting patiently at Horse Guards, were soaked to the skin. Given those circumstances, no Colonel-in-Chief worth her salt sends for something to keep her dry.

So the Queen and her royal aides-de-camp sat it out as the rain poured down, and at one point it bucketed down so unbelievably hard that the Queen found it impossible to contain her amusement (top, and above). It may have detracted from the supposed solemnity of the occasion, but it was a forgiveable lapse on the Queen's part. After all, what quirk of destiny should have left her here, sitting on a horse in a rainstorm, watching armies of grown men trying to march briskly past in uniforms doubled in weight by gallons of water? It was enough to make a horse laugh.

Not many people were laughing at Horse Guards Parade. The stands erected for successive performances of Beating the Retreat earlier that week now housed thousands of people in summer clothes getting helplessly and irretrievably drenched. Normally there is an all too obvious distinction between spectators loyally wearing uniform, those who treat the occasion as sufficiently dressy to wear their finer clothes and those casually dressed in denims and open-necked shirts. This morning, in the blur of such an enormous downpour, the only distinction was between those who had brought rainwear and those who hadn't.

For once there was no time or appetite to savour the Palladian Islands could not possibly have been as bad as this.

The Queen was making her way down the Mall, preceded by the Brigadier Major of the Coldstreams on his 38th birthday, four troopers of the Blues and Royals, the massed bands (48 musicians from the Blues and Royals and Life Guards) and two divisions of the Sovereign's Escort – 96 men all told. With the Queen rode three Princes of the Blood Royal – the Duke of Edinburgh as Colonel of the Grenadier Guards, riding the carriage-horse Solomon;

Horse Guards Building was deliberately held back, if necessary, to allow for lateness so that it invariably chimed just as the Queen's horse set foot on the parade ground. But that meticulously informed television commentator, Richard Dimbleby, divulged the details of this practice on one occasion early in the 1960's and the Queen ordered that it should be discontinued forthwith. Nevertheless she still manages to arrive punctually, and she did so again this year. As if by the same magic touch that was once believed to cure scrofula, the rain stopped and the sun appeared, picking out gleaming medals and the bright Garter Sash and Star on her now glistening scarlet tunic and the proud, full red plume on her black tricorne hat. That red plume signified her role for the day – Colonel-in-Chief of the Coldstream Guards whose Colour was being trooped today. And the National Anthem which greeted her arrival signalled the

Prince Charles as Colonel of the Welsh Guards, riding Centennial, the black gelding he had ridden in the Silver Jubilee procession; the Duke of Kent, Colonel of the Scots Guards, riding Richard, the grey police horse (above).

Trooping the Colour is traditionally a spectacle enjoyed by the whole of the Queen's family and, despite the weather, this was no exception. Thus members of the Royal Family not taking part in the parade, including the Princess of Wales, arrived by car via Whitehall to watch from the balconied window of the Horse Guards Building. The more seasoned senior members, the Queen Mother and Princess Margaret had left Buckingham Palace at 10.40 in a covered barouche (opposite page bottom left) accompanied by the Duke of Beaufort, former Master of the Queen's Horse. Number Three Guard broke ranks to allow their carriage and that of their attendants through as six bars of the National Anthem floated towards them.

Ten minutes later, on the stroke of eleven, the Queen arrived. It is no longer known how coincidental with the precise hour the Queen's arrival is. Time was when the clock above

beginning of a great occasion for the Coldstreams.

For the first time in ten years – since the death of the Duke of Windsor in 1972 – the ceremony was preceded by a minute's silence, to remember the two hundred or more, many from regiments now on parade, killed in nine weeks of battles for the Falkland Islands. For as the distant thud of King's Troop guns booming their Birthday salute in Hyde Park broke the eerie silence, it was worth remembering that this spectacular ceremony was merely the pleasant side of the life of a Guardsman, and that the

"Les Huguenots" which has been played at this point in the parade since 1869, and which involves almost every instrument known to military bands, from piccolos to euphoniums.

In another long-established move, practised since 1759, a lone drummer detached himself from his regiment and marched out to give the drum signal to troop, and the Escort to the Colour, comprising three officers and 70 other ranks, marched across the parade to receive the Colour. Despite the fact that it was the Coldstream Guards' Colour, the tune to which they now marched was the traditional

Welsh and Scots Guards were even now on the Falklands, the Irish Guards in Germany, and the Coldstreams themselves bound for Northern Ireland in September. Nevertheless, the ceremony was not reduced or curtailed – there was the usual complement of 56 officers and 1,379 men on parade, including 445 lining the processional route.

The only woman on parade was the Queen, and she began the hour-long ceremony by inspecting, on horseback, her troops to a slow march "La Plume Rouge" followed by a quick march "Sussex by the Sea." As she returned to the saluting base the order for the Troop was given and, headed by five drum majors, the massed bands marched and counter-marched to the well known air

"British Grenadiers." The Escort stopped ten paces away from the Colour and Regimental Sergeant John Pratt, now celebrating 21 of his 39 years in the Army, took it from Sergeant David Blenkinsop and positioned it in a sheath in the belt of the Ensign for the Colour, Second Lieutenant Andrew Pickthorn, whose job it now was to carry it in this uncomfortable position throughout most of the rest of the ceremony, and back to barracks afterwards – a total of almost two hours. The most excruciating moment of all, as for all bearers of the Colour on this occasion, would come at the precise moment of the Troop when it was to be lowered as it passed the Queen. The sheer weight of the standard, manoeuvred by the movement of one hand, wrist and arm concentrated on the lowest part of the pole, makes the moment a supreme test of nerve and muscular strength.

Then, to the slow march "Escort to the Colour," the heavy, ornamental flag on its 8½ foot long pole was trooped through the ranks, a symbolic reminder of the ceremony's origin – the raising of the regimental flag at the rallying point to indicate to billetted soldiers where they had to meet. It was 177 years since the flag was trooped on the monarch's birthday: George III was the first to be so honoured in 1805.

Large sections of the seven thousand strong audience stood as the Colour passed them. This particular Colour bore 43 battle honours, from Oudenarde to Salerno, out of the 111 so far awarded to the regiment, and the Garter Star and portrait of the Sphinx almost shone out from the deep crimson background. The Queen, before whom it was now to be trooped, had presented it to the regiment at Windsor in 1976.

The Queen has taken the Salute every year but one since she deputised for her father King George VI in 1951, and did so again as the Colour was lowered

before her for the thirty-first time. For her it was almost routine, but for the ever-changing personnel of the Guards it all requires two months' practice and two major rehearsals. Every movement of the entire march-past of six double ranks of Guards (opposite page, top and bottom right) had to be correct or, it is rumoured, their Colonel-in-Chief will want to know why. In a movement first introduced

into the ceremony by King George VI in 1949, the Household Cavalry, who had been rooted to the spot for almost an hour, ranked past the Queen, first at the walk and then, after a trumpeter's signal, at the trot. The jingling mass of harnesses and glinting helmets and cuirasses was led by the two enormous drum-horses – Coriolanus, the nine-year-old presented by the Queen, and Caractacus, the eleven-year-old

skewbald, whose first Queen's Birthday Parade this was. Each carried a drummer and a pair of priceless and irreplaceable drums given by George III in 1803 and William IV in 1830, their solid silver bulk weighing half a hundredweight each.

The rank and file horses had already had a long morning. As in each year, they were saddled up and ready by 9.30, and had been stood to the groom for five or six hours the previous day. The majority of them were bred in Ireland and are between four and sixteen years of age, but Ophelia is proudly in her 25th year. And the names of the horses – which are a minimum of sixteen hands high – vary with the year in which they are introduced. Like cars, whose registration letters proclaim their year of registration, the horses' initials change each year.

This year the new horses were all given names beginning with H.

JUNE 1982

The ceremony was now nearing its end, and it was time for the royal spectators to make a move. Almost unnoticed, the Queen Mother and the rest of the Royal Family disappeared from their vantage point and filed into cars which drove them back in procession towards Buckingham Palace. On the parade ground, original positions were regained by the Household Cavalry and, on receiving a well-rehearsed signal that the Queen Mother's procession was in the Mall, and the Colonel of the Coldstream Guards, Michael Maxey, rode to within earshot of the Queen to inform her that "Your Majesty's Guards are ready to move off, Ma'am." The Queen nodded her approval, as she always does, and the march-off began. As a tribute to their Scots and Welsh Guards colleagues, the unusual decision was made to play

"Hi'land Laddie" and "The Rising of the Lark" for this final part of this almost unchanging, but never tired, ceremony. So off went the Queen and her aides at the head of her troops. The tradition of Sovereign leading Guards back to the Palace was commenced by King George V in 1914, just three years after the magnificent Queen Victoria Memorial, past which they would all process, was completed and unveiled in the presence of the Kaiser, the man who put the Trooping into khaki until 1921. It is a symbolic gesture, much admired by the thousands of spectators – tourists from all parts of the

fly past. The photograph left shows, from left to right, the Queen, whose waving hand is obscuring Princess Alice, Duchess of Gloucester, in front of Prince Michael of Kent; then Princess Alexandra, Prince Philip, Mr Angus Ogilvy, the Princess of Wales, the Duke of Kent and his younger son Lord Nicholas Windsor. The Queen Mother, Princess Margaret, the Duke and Duchess of Gloucester with their elder children the Earl of Ulster and Lady Davina Windsor, the Duchess of Kent, and Princess Michael were also there.

Thus was this stylish ritual, incorporating over two centuries of royal and military history, brought to its end.

It has remained as popular as ever, thanks to the sheer efficiency and smartness of the Guards, and to the fact that for forty-five years it has been held

world and citizens of London alike – who enjoy the sight as living evidence of the Queen's titular leadership of her forces. One concession to circumstances was made. After the incident in June 1981 in which blank shots were fired at the Queen in the Mall, the point at which this happened was cordoned off so that ten feet of empty pavement separated the road from the front of the crowd. It was realised that the narrowness of the approach road, which leads off the Mall at that point, brought the Queen too close to would-be assailants.

To-day's ceremonies were unmarred by any such occurrences and the Queen reached Buckingham Palace safely, if somewhat soggily. And with the experience of that very wet start to the day receding, she and the rest of the Royal Family came out onto the balcony to witness and acknowledge the Royal Air Force's own birthday tribute, the traditional and noisy as a fixed annual spectacle, on the second Saturday in June, regardless of the actual date of the Sovereign's birthday. By that token, the best of the year's weather is always assured. Well, nearly always.

There were no new Knights of the Order of the Garter to be invested this year, so the Throne Room of Windsor Castle was bereft of ceremony on 14th June. But there was a meeting of the Order, as usual, and a luncheon at which all the Knights taking part in the afternoon's service were present, along with the officers of the Order and the pages.

If it is ever permissible to talk of the Garter ceremony as low-key, this year's proceedings fitted that description. Relatively speaking of course. The ceremonial is in essence as spectacular, the

colour as vivid, the applause as warm as always, but there was no doubt that some earlier ceremonies had the edge. The buzz of speculation centred first and foremost on the Princess of Wales: she was here last year as Lady Diana Spencer – would she attend again today in her new capacity? Spectators craned their necks and swore they'd seen her, but in fact she never appeared. No foreign royalty either. Two years ago both the Queen of Denmark and the Grand Duke of Luxemburg had attended, to add their own brand of informality on the

windswept steps of St George's Chapel. Today it was as if King Farouk's prophecy – "One day there will be only five kings left – of Britain, hearts, clubs, diamonds and spades" – had come true.

Even the Duke of Edinburgh was absent: at short notice he had left London Airport that morning to attend the funeral of King Khalid of Saudi Arabia – a State Visitor to Britain in 1981 – who had died the previous day, and to pay his respects and convey the Queen's condolences to his brother and successor Crown-Prince Faud.

Thus, for once, the Queen walked alone in the procession which formed inside the Castle and snaked down the Grand Staircase to the Grand Entrance where the ten Military Knights of Windsor, in scarlet tunics with white sashes, and the thirteen tabarded heralds and pursuivants joined to form the vanguard of the procession. Between them and the Sovereign came eighteen

JUNE 1982

Knights, incredibly resplendent in their heavy, rich, blue mantles and white plumes shifting restlessly in a stiffish, though by no means unpleasant breeze. Sir Harold Wilson – one of the few recognisable faces, or names for that matter – waved cheerily, even royally. He was the only one to do so, as if all the applause were being accorded exclusively to him. The Knights were followed by the Queen Mother, with the Prince of Wales as her escort, and the applause grew pointedly louder.

The Queen, her face almost framed by the sweeping lines of

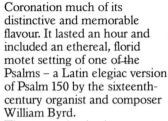

Coronation much of its distinctive and memorable flavour. It lasted an hour and included an ethereal, florid motet setting of one of the Psalms – a Latin elegiac version of Psalm 150 by the sixteenth-century organist and composer William Byrd.

The procession back was more, and less, spectacular than the arrival. More, because the Royal Family used carriages to take them back up the hill to the Castle: the Queen was joined by the Prince of Wales, the Queen Mother by the Duke of Beaufort. Less, because the

her plumed cap, looked defiantly young and palpably happy in the leisurely walk towards St George's Chapel as, section by section, the thousands of spectators, ticket-holders and invitees, rose to applaud her as they had done her mother and son. Soldiers of the Life Guards and the Blues and Royals, distinguishable by their white and red plumes respectively, studded the route on either side.

The service was relayed to those outside through unseen loudspeakers, and was full of the sounds – like Walton's *Te Deum* and Gordon Jacob's National Anthem – which gave the

Rome, nor the demotion by the Vatican of the Order's patron saint, St George, nor the scepticism of a generation speeding on towards the twenty-first century, have diminished the pleasurable tradition of its annual celebration.

The week ushered in by the splendour of the Garter ceremony continued with splendour of another kind, difficult to regard as formal and official, but as inescapably British as any military parade. On the Tuesday following Garter Day and for the three remaining days of the week, the eyes of the horse-racing fraternity were turned to, and fixed on, Royal Ascot.

Not only the horse-racing fraternity of course. Royal Ascot is as synonymous with hats as with horses and the expectation of four days of seeing and being seen on Ascot's sweeping course-side lawns or in its

Knights, few of them in the flower of youth, took cars. And eventually the Guards arranged themselves back into units and marched off as well.

Edward III had, for most of his comparatively long life, a sense of proportion, and would have been more than surprised to know that the Order of the Garter which, according to legend, he founded after picking up a lady's garter and placing it, jokingly, upon his own leg, was still alive and flourishing in the dying years of the twentieth century. Neither the breach with

fashionable bars and restaurants is as likely to draw any socialite or sartorial expert as is the opportunity to be in the unsaddling enclosure when the Gold Cup winner comes in.

Any venture into the social scene in Britain leads to excess and the unavoidable juggernaut of commercial marketing makes it chic to run publicity stunts against the respectable and respected Ascot background. Thus the camera crews are always looking for Mrs Shilling in her outrageous creations, or spying on some advertising

Anne who directed the laying-out of the Ascot course almost three hundred years ago and the presence of her equally enthusiastic successor today symbolises the continuing, though not unbroken, equestrian sympathies for which the Royal Family is well-known.

The Queen's continued patronage of the event also embodies a social statement of precedence and authority within that now amorphous section of society which is content to look to her for an indefinable leadership, an annual stamp of approval and encouragement for

agency's furtive attempts to place models in the correct setting as they brandish glasses of wine, sport summer fashions or purse lips caked with the latest cosmetic preparation.

It is hard to see where the Royal Family might fit into this, but its members enter into the four-day festival with as much gusto, in their restrained royal way, as anyone. It was of course Queen

the respectable in a world where respectability enjoys a declining role.

The grand entrance and arrival say it all. A line of carriages bowls at casual pace through Ascot's famous Golden Gates and an unstoppable surge of people rushes towards the rails for a fleeting glimpse of the procession, thin and silent in an immensely wide expanse of turf, being hauled by. Similarly, a crowd of spectators in the Royal Enclosure makes way for the royal progress on foot to the Royal Box in the Queen Elizabeth II Stand, and the front

Queen Mother looking like – well, looking like the Queen Mother, in her favourite pale coats and chiffon dresses. Prince Philip missed out on Tuesday and Friday; Princess Margaret wore her azalea Royal Wedding outfit and made nonsense of the rumours that she is no friend of the éclatante Princess Michael (opposite page, centre), and it was so very easy to see why the Duchess of Kent has been described as one of the seven most sophisticated women in the world.

lines of ladies in competing hats compete also for the chance to catch the royal eye (opposite page, bottom right).

From 15th to 18th June the ritual was enacted again before crowds whose numbers promised to exceed the record. More hopes of seeing the Princess of Wales perhaps? If so they were disappointed. On no day did she join the carriage procession and only on one did she slip quietly into the Royal Box, having arrived unobtrusively by car. In fact there was no day when the Family was wholly represented. The Queen and Queen Mother attended on all four days, the Queen looking particularly chic in a beige-coloured scalloped coat and matching hat, and the

JUNE 1982

Royal Ascot week must be a quietly satisfying time for the Royal Family. Its female members clearly enjoy the elegance and traditions of this most social of race meetings, while for its male members, who might understandably tire of an excess of seeing and being seen, a rival attraction close by offers a

chance to escape, and action of a more competitive kind.

Just five miles from Ascot race course lies Smiths Lawn in Windsor Great Park, and on each of the four days of Royal Ascot, polo matches were arranged during the late afternoon and evening so that racegoers could finish off their day's racing with a look at the polo.

Prince Charles, who was not conspicuous at Ascot this year, continued to give much of his leisure time to polo, and on 18th June he was playing for Galen Weston's Maple Leaf team for

the Mountbatten Cup. It seems that the discussions he had before the match with Major Ronald Ferguson, his polo manager (below and far left) were useful because Maple Leaf ended the day victorious and Prince Charles, who captained the side, received the winning

August at Windsor Great Park, where he competed for the Jaipur Trophy. In this match he scored a goal but his reputation for falling off horses lost nothing as his mount, a six-year-old pony called Cinderella, threw him over the top in a closely fought scramble for the ball. The Prince fell heavily, was severely winded and sat for a minute seeming completely dazed. He rather lost his temper with the pony but the accident was probably due to the fact that he was unaccustomed to riding her. He had put all his own ponies out to grass and Cinderella belonged to the Queen.

During July Prince Charles

continued to play for his other team, Les Diables Bleus, in the British Open Championships at Cowdray Park, in the Cowdray Park Gold Cup, and for England's B Team in Cup matches at Windsor.

team's blue rosette and a personal prize from the Queen, who had by then changed from her Ascot dress into something a little less formal (opposite page, top). The Queen also presented prizes to the other three members of the team (right and above right) as well as consolation prizes to the losers (far right).

Prince Charles' association with Maple Leaf this season was a fruitful one. He was playing for them again on 2nd August, just two days before Prince William's christening, and again on 8th

JUNE 1982

When the Queen landed at RAF Wittering on the morning of 21st June, her daughter-in-law had been in hospital for over five hours awaiting the birth of the heir, after Prince Charles, to the Throne. As Her Majesty's visit itself was scheduled to last a further five hours, a special radio link was set up in the Queen's Andover to catch any news of the Princess of Wales' progress. The Queen showed no sign of preoccupation or lack of interest in the event she had come to witness – a programme of displays and exhibitions to celebrate the fortieth anniversary of the Royal Air Force Regiment. The invitation was originally to the Queen alone, but the Duke of Edinburgh asked if he could come too. There was no resisting the double distinction.

It was King George VI who in 1942 signed the Royal Warrant which founded the Regiment. Its purpose, then as now, was to safeguard military airfields from the kind of air attacks which in the early years of the war threatened to annihilate Britain's

already outnumbered air strike capabilities. By 1944 it had covered not only all major airfields in Britain, but had been engaged in North Africa, Italy, the Balkans and eventually the Far East, and more recent service in all parts of the world from Central America to the

Persian Gulf emphasise its continuing importance. The Queen and the Duke's arrival was marked by a ceremonial parade of the Regiment which the Queen inspected from the comfort and shelter, on a cool, blowy day, of a Range Rover (left). She then took the Salute as the Queen's Colour for the Regiment was trooped through the squadrons to music, some of which, like Verdi's "Aida," featured in the Trooping the Colour ceremony in London nine days before. A somewhat more spectacular salute, in the form of a flypast by

six Tornadoes (borrowed from RAF Honington) and six Jaguars (from RAF Coltishall), followed, before the royal couple were taken towards a hangar where they saw an exhibition covering the forty-year history of the Regiment (previous page right). The display which ensued demonstrated the current roles and capabilities of the Regiment

as a support unit for air operations, and brought home graphically the importance of such a unit in a conflict like that which had just ended in the Falklands. It opened with a drop of paratroops who then drove the "enemy" from an aircraft strip, while enemy mortar fire was suppressed by RAF Harrier jump-jets. Light armoured vehicles were then landed by Hercules and Chinooks and the efficacy of the Rapiers in the Falklands was clearly shown as their fire units tracked a simulated enemy air attack. A subsequent enemy attack was countered by mobile Regimental forces, and two Harriers landed safely at base in front of the Queen.

Then came the gentler business of meeting the families of RAF personnel (these pages), when the Queen received a bouquet from six-year-old Pauline Phillips, and of being introduced to Flight Lieutenant "Danny" Gourd who after nearly 41 years' service is the last serving founder member of the Regiment. But perhaps the going home was, for once, best. There were urgent family matters to attend to.

JUNE 1982

As it turned out, family matters were not as urgent as all that. The Princess of Wales' admission into St Mary's Hospital Paddington was inconspicuous as no other of her

But the lengthy labour gave time for the public to express its best wishes and before long, bottles of champagne, toys and flowers – of which this beautifully arranged basket (bottom centre) was the best example – were being delivered to hospital staff at the Lindo Wing. Crowds arrived; few left and most stayed, more determined as the minutes ticked by to justify their efforts by hanging on for the final *dénouement*.

Eventually, of course, it happened. At precisely 9.03 pm on Monday 21st June, the Queen's first grandson in direct male line of succession was born. The cheers went up outside St Mary's and at Buckingham

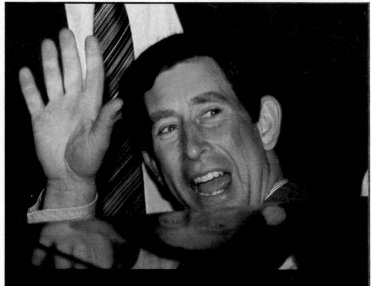

activities over the previous year and a half had been, and Britain woke up excitedly to the prospect of a royal birth before lunch-time. But that was like saying that the First World War would be over by Christmas. To those waiting at a distance for the news, the day seemed to drag on.

lipstick on his cheek (opposite page), and disappeared to Kensington for a good night's sleep. The Queen could not conceal her joy the following day (opposite page top and bottom right) and Lord Spencer was as proud as Punch (opposite page top left). Mrs Shand Kydd said, "There's a lot of happiness up there."

That afternoon the happiness came down to ground level, Prince Charles, significantly, holding his son as he first appeared before his future subjects. Radiance, pride, contentment – all those royal clichés – seemed inadequate in the general rejoicing.

Palace where the customary bulletin (top right) was secured to the gates; champagne corks popped all over the country; Fleet Street went wild with congratulations and various members of the Royal Family pronounced themselves delighted in one degree or another.

Prince Charles emerged at 11.15 triumphant, talkative and with

JULY 1982

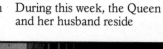

Like all other members of the Royal Family, the Queen and Prince Philip pay several visits to Scotland in the course of the year, in addition to the long summer holiday at Balmoral and their occasional Spring weekends there. It has long been a custom, however, for them to spirit was enormously helped by the installation of the railways, of which she made such comprehensive use that the steam engine might seem to have been invented specifically for her.

During this week, the Queen and her husband reside

acknowledge this part of the kingdom by a special week-long visit, with each day packed with engagements taking them to all parts of the lowlands. This practice has its origins in Queen Victoria's reign. Her personal love of Scotland prompted her to make frequent visits north of the Border, and her pioneering

permanently at their official residence in Scotland, the Palace of Holyroodhouse, and the Queen's personal bodyguard for the duration is the three hundred-year-old Royal Company of Archers. Scotland, which was the first part of the United Kingdom

Cathedral Edinburgh at which two new Knights of the Order of the Thistle were installed – Lord Elgin and Lord Thompson. The Service, which is an annual one, took place in the Order's Chapel which occupies a small extension to the Cathedral, and the ceremonial included the

formation of the Royal Company of Archers as the Queen's bodyguard, and music from the band of the Gordon Highlanders.

The visual impact of the Thistle ceremony (this page) is similar to that of the Garter, although the surroundings – Parliament

Square in Edinburgh – are not so imposing as Windsor Castle. But the rich, flowing robes are there, the handsome white plumes are there, and the long stately procession of Knights follows a pattern similar to the Windsor ceremony. Unlike Windsor, however, the Thistle service is held in the morning, with the traditional luncheon taking place at Holyroodhouse afterwards.

The Order of the Thistle has its roots in the 15th century, but Queen Anne made the last of several revivals in 1703.

officially to greet the Queen during her Silver Jubilee tour of 1977, always looks forward to these days each year when the Sovereign's attention is concentrated solely on matters north of the Border. At no time is the excitement and sense of national identity greater than when the royal couple attend the Pipers' Ball and the great ceremonies of the Order of the Thistle.

This year the Pipers' Ball, or the Royal Scottish Pipers' Society Ball, to give it its full name, celebrated its centenary and the Assembly Rooms in royal Edinburgh looked especially festive. The Queen and Prince Philip are seen (left) arriving, on 2nd July, accompanied by the Chairman of the Centenary Committee, and (centre left) with Sir James Morrison-Low, the Society's Honorary Pipe-Major.

Earlier that day the Queen and Duke of Edinburgh had attended a service in St Giles'

JULY 1982

There was a busy schedule for the Queen and the Duke of Edinburgh in Scotland. On 29th June the Queen gave audiences at Holyroodhouse before visiting George Watson's College in Edinburgh (bottom pictures) where she attended a concert and saw one schoolboy preparing to make clay models of each member of the Royal Family (bottom right). She also attended a Regimental Dinner of the Royal Scots Dragoon Guards.

The following day the Queen opened the Biochemistry Department at the Moredun Institute (right and below) and

gave a garden party at Holyroodhouse. She had previously visited a Micro-Electronics Institute.
On 1st July there were visits to the Royal and Ancient Golf Club, and St Andrew's

University. The Queen and Duke watched the launching of a new lifeboat (below) during an enthusiastically received visit to Anstruther (far left), before going to Methil and Glenrothes. Subsequent engagements included a reception for the Duke of Edinburgh Award winners which Prince Philip attended (bottom pictures) on 2nd July in between his visits to the Royal Scottish Academy and his tour of the new Church Halls in Leith, and a visit to the Forres Games on 3rd July (opposite page, top right).

"The British, bless them, do hate emotion," said Harold Nicolson. He would hardly have recognised the British character amid the scenes of immense jubilation and poignancy which

who had sailed in the *Queen Elizabeth 2*.

Her owners and crew were more than proud of the fact that during the whole of the expedition the *Canberra* never once suffered a mechanical failure and that her indispensible services included everything from housing Argentine prisoners to accepting survivors from the sinking of *HMS Ardent*. It all involved an enormous transformation from her normal peace-time activities: not only was she fitted with two helicopter pads during the short space of three days between her last cruise and her spell of military duty; she also served 650,000 meals and produced almost 40,000 tons of fresh water while in service – a huge increase on anything she is called upon to supply for the

surrounded the glorious return of the *SS Canberra* from the Falkland Islands on 11th July. The *Canberra* came back to Southampton, the port she had sailed from on 9th April as part of the Task Force sent by the Government to the South Atlantic. She was almost eighteen weeks at sea and travelled over 27,000 miles in that time. She was under air attack for ten hours while disembarking her 2,000 troops at San Carlos, where the British forces established their first beachhead on the mainland of the Falklands, and she was sent back to San Carlos to transfer a further complement of soldiers

purpose of normal leisure cruises. And in those eighteen weeks over half a million man-miles had been run round her promenade deck.

The Prince of Wales, who only five days earlier had received members of the Parachute Regiment as they returned to RAF Brize Norton from the

welcomings began. As *Canberra* finally berthed, the troops erupted in a frenzy of shouting and singing (left and bottom left) to match the emotional celebration of thanksgiving awaiting their disembarkation. The scenes were nothing short of spectacular and the

Falklands, now decided to travel to Southampton to welcome the *Canberra* home. Understanding that for many of the men and for their families waiting on the quays at Southampton, this would be a very private homecoming, he resolved that his presence should not detract from the spontaneity of personal reunions. So he piloted his own helicopter aboard *Canberra* (opposite page top left) before she berthed, and left while she was still manoeuvring into Southampton Water (far left). Once aboard, he met Lt-General Sir Steuart Pringle of the Royal Marines (opposite page top right) and went below decks to

talk to some of the men who saw and returned from active service (opposite page left). These included Marine Chris Goodwill of 45 Commando who suffered gunshot wounds at Two Sisters – which many regarded as the most frightening phase of the conflict – and Marine Stephen Chubb of 42 Commando who was wounded at Mount Harriet.

As Prince Charles left, an army of private boats swarmed round (above left), as national

enthusiasm of those on ship and quayside alike increased as the long process of offloading continued. The cheering went on, unabated, for hours while mothers, wives and girlfriends wept effusively as they caught sight of their menfolk for the first time in fourteen weeks. Prince Charles summed it all up. "I am delighted to be able to do something small to welcome these people back. They have done the most fantastic job."

JULY 1982

No one member of the Royal Family became so readily or so fully associated with the Falklands conflict as seen from home base, as it were, as the Prince of Wales. With his own brother involved in the heat of the battle for the Islands' recapture, his appreciation of the problems of serving men and their relatives was keen and sincere. His close interest in the Task Force was shown time and again as he waited at airfields to welcome home members of the

Royal Navy, entered the Royal Box, which was encrusted in flowers of blue, green and white, the colours of the new South Atlantic Ribbon, to a fanfare by the State Trumpeters, before Lord Olivier came onto the stage to preface the evening's entertainment. He referred, in an implacable foreword, to "the avaricious intentions" of the Argentine against the Falklands and the valour of the men who saved the islands.

Then came a succession of

artistes from the entire world of entertainment – comedians, singers, dancers, pop groups, ballet dancers, massed bands and operatic groups. The generation of stars who entertained during the Second World War were represented by Dame Vera Lynn (talking to Prince Charles, opposite page far right, with Tommy Steele) and the actress Dame Anna Neagle (below), while the younger generation of contemporary entertainers

Parachute Regiment, visited the casualties in hospitals, and spoke to the families of those who waited and hoped.

With the report of the first of the 250 or so fatal casualties of the Falkland Islands conflict, a South Atlantic Fund was established to help the bereaved families and the dependents of those badly injured on active service. The Prince of Wales agreed in June to become Patron of the Fund and on 18th July he attended a glittering variety show entitled "National Salute to the Falklands Task Force" at the London Coliseum.

Over 100 artistes – there were some thirty individual contributions alone – gave their services free of charge: Lord Goodman and Prince Charles' cousin, Lord Harewood, put the theatre at the organisers' disposal, and the televising of the show by London Weekend Television gave the Fund an additional, incalcuable financial boost.

The Prince, dressed in the uniform of a Commander in the

included Twiggy and Adam Ant (opposite page, bottom pictures, with Dickie Henderson). Alfred Marks, Billy Dainty, Leslie Crowther and Danny la Rue were also there as well as Ronnie Corbett and Paul Daniels. After the show, Prince Charles met the entire company, including the naval ratings (opposite page, centre left) who had joined in the finale in which Dame Vera Lynn led 300 performers in the singing of

"Land of Hope and Glory," and troops from the Gurkha Regiment (bottom left). He spoke to Roger Moore and Les Dawson (opposite page far right). "Any chance of payment?" said Dawson. "We want more security." Prince Charles looked at Roger Moore: "He's got terrible habits," he' told him.

The Prince spoke to former Goon Harry Secombe and wanted to know whether he was

"keeping his knees up." He also met Jimmy Tarbuck who, during the show, wanted to know why the Queen's wisdom tooth – she had been operated on the week before – had gone undetected for so long. "There'll be questions in the House," he warned, in a clear reference to the affair of the Palace intruder.

The show had lasted a full three hours and was a tremendous success. Over 2,500 people had paid up to £100 each for tickets and with television rights and contributions the entire evening produced a profit of almost £½ million for the Fund. Its Patron (left, meeting Lord Olivier after the show) was overwhelmed. "Marvellous," he said. "Just marvellous." No wonder Mr John Nott (top left, behind Prince Charles) who in April had offered his resignation as Defence Secretary, looked pleased.

JULY 1982

The Duke of Kent, Grand Master of the Order of St Michael and St George, attended the Order's annual Service at St Paul's Cathedral on 20th July (below). The Duke usually attends with the Duchess of Kent but this year presided alone, wearing the colourful blue mantle of the Order with its superb Star and Chain. The Queen, as Sovereign of the Order, has not attended an Annual Service for some years. The Queen Mother, following Prince Charles' patronage of Operation Drake, saw the barge *Dannebrog* during her visit to

London Gardens Society. On July 14th she visited gardens in Kensington (left and below) and Wandsworth. Her own enthusiasm for gardening developed when she and the late King George VI took over Royal Lodge Windsor in the 1930's, transforming it from virtual jungle to the colourful gardens that exist today.

There was a breezy reception for the Queen at Mill Hill on 16th July, when, as Colonel-in-Chief of the Royal Engineers, she visited the Postal Branch of the Corps which was celebrating its centenary. The visit, which

the Fellowship of St Katherine's Dock in London on 22nd July (above).

Perhaps the Queen Mother's favourite public engagement is her annual visit to prizewinning gardens in the London area under the auspices of the

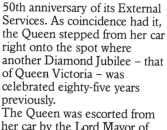

50th anniversary of its External Services. As coincidence had it, the Queen stepped from her car right onto the spot where another Diamond Jubilee – that of Queen Victoria – was celebrated eighty-five years previously.

The Queen was escorted from her car by the Lord Mayor of London (left) and entered the Cathedral to Sir Arthur Bliss' Fanfare for Heroes. During the service, a montage of sound was presented, in which the Queen and Prince Philip heard the voices of King George V, King George VI and that of the

included a luncheon in the Officers' Mess, was concluded by a reception in the garden of the headquarters (opposite page, bottom pictures). By coincidence Prince Philip was at the same time visiting the Intelligence Corps in Leicestershire.

St Paul's Cathedral was again the venue for a royal visit when on 12th July the Queen and Prince Philip attended a service there to commemorate two of the BBC's perennial anniversaries – the Diamond Jubilee of its foundation and the

Queen herself, as the history of the BBC was encapsulated in this fifteen minute summary in sound. The service ended unusually, with leaders of six different faiths – Hindu, Sikh, Muslim, Buddhist, Jewish and Christian giving their own versions of the Peace Blessing, in fulfilment of the BBC's motto "Nation Shall Speak Peace Unto Nation."

The Queen showed no sign of unease after the revelation that morning that a man had entered her bedroom at Buckingham Palace. Nor did Commander Michael Trestrail (top left) for whom, in the indirect wake of that revelation, this was to be the last public appearance as the Queen's police officer.